A guide for
a successful career
in science

GEORGIOS KOUBOURIS

DEDICATION

This book is dedicated to my family for providing continuous and unconditional support and for being a source of inspiration for me. I also dedicate this book to every person dreaming of contributing to society through science.

ACKNOWLEDGMENTS

I would like to thank from the bottom of my heart all of the people I have interacted with throughout my life and who shaped my personality to be able to write this book and share it with you. A big thank you is ought also to you for aiming at self-improvement and life-long learning.

CONTENTS

Preface

It is fascinating to realize that science has been at the forefront of human progress for centuries, constantly pushing the boundaries of knowledge and understanding. From discovering the laws of physics that govern the universe to developing new technologies that have revolutionized our daily lives, scientists have been the driving force behind some of the greatest achievements in human history.

I guess we have all wondered, what exactly does it mean to be a scientist? What are the skills and qualities that make someone successful in this profession? What are the challenges and rewards of a career in science?

This book aims to answer these questions and more by delving into the fascinating world of science and the people who pursue it. Through a combination of personal stories and research, we will explore the diverse paths that scientists take, from academia to industry to government, and the varied fields of study that they specialize in, from biology to physics to engineering. We also delve into the day-to-day work of scientists, from designing experiments to analyzing data to presenting findings, and the skills that are essential for success in this field, such as critical thinking, communication, and persistence.

But we should keep in mind that being a scientist is not just about technical skills and knowledge. It also requires creativity, curiosity, and a passion for discovery. We explore the personal motivations that drive scientists, the challenges they face, and the impact that their work can have on society.

I am confident that whether you are a student considering a career in science or a seasoned professional looking to learn more about your field, this book will provide a comprehensive and engaging exploration of the profession of scientists. I suggest that you use this book as a work tool. Keep it with you at all times and read it again and again. Consider it as your life coach!

1 TO BECOME OR NOT TO BECOME A SCIENTIST?

I cannot stress enough that selecting a profession can be a difficult task, as it involves choosing a career path that will shape one's life. Usually, this decision is taken at an early age, when we don't have enough information and experience to support a certain decision. It is not extreme to say that many people end up doing a job at random. This may have serious implications in life, leading to high job dissatisfaction rates and career changes that require an additional investment in effort, time, and funding for training in the new discipline.

I guess that we all agree that the decision to become a scientist requires careful consideration, as it demands a unique set of skills, passions, and commitments. In this chapter, we will discuss why someone might choose to become a scientist and explore the various factors that contribute to this decision.

A fundamental feature of scientists is that they are driven by a deep sense of curiosity and a passion for learning. They are constantly seeking to understand the world around them and are not satisfied with surface-level explanations. For many people, the thrill of discovery is what draws them to the field of science. They want to uncover new information and make breakthroughs that will contribute to the advancement of knowledge.

We can be sure that the pursuit of scientific discovery is an intellectually challenging endeavor. It requires creativity, critical thinking, and problem-solving skills. Scientists must be able to analyze complex data and draw meaningful conclusions from it. They must also be able to communicate their findings effectively, both to their peers and to the general public. For those who enjoy mental stimulation and are motivated by intellectual challenges, a career in science can be an excellent fit.

Furthermore, a motivation for becoming a scientist is that science has the potential to make a significant impact on the world. Through scientific research, we have been able to develop new technologies, create life-saving drugs, and solve some of the most pressing problems facing humanity. For those who are driven by a desire to make a difference in the world, a career in science can offer ample opportunities for innovation and impact.

Of course, we should keep in mind that science is not a solitary pursuit. It requires collaboration with other scientists, both within and across disciplines. Scientists often work in teams to tackle complex problems, and the sense of community that develops within the scientific community can be a powerful motivator. For those who enjoy working with others and value a sense of belonging, a career in science can offer a supportive and collaborative environment.

Let's remember that science is a vast field, with many different specializations and career paths. This diversity means that scientists have a great deal of flexibility in choosing their career trajectories. They may choose to work in academia, government, or industry, or they may pursue careers in science communication, or policy. Scientists also have the opportunity to travel and work in different parts of the world, as scientific research is a global enterprise. For those who value flexibility and mobility, a career in science can offer a great deal of variety and opportunity.

In the end, I would say that choosing to become a scientist is not a decision that should be taken lightly. It requires a significant commitment of time, energy, and resources. However, for those who are driven by curiosity, intellectual challenge, a desire to make a difference, and a sense of community, a career in science can be immensely rewarding. I am sure that you would agree that with opportunities for innovation, impact, and mobility, science is a field that offers ample opportunities for personal and professional growth. Last but not least, scientists commonly have a high satisfaction rate regarding their jobs and are rarely bored because they continuously search for new findings and solutions to problems.

2 COMMON PROBLEMS FACED BY SCIENTISTS

We have discussed some exciting aspects of starting a career in the scientific world. However, let's keep in mind that science is fascinating but is not free from all problems. It is an ever-evolving field that is full of challenges and opportunities. Scientists are constantly working to discover new information, understand complex phenomena, and develop new technologies. Though, this journey is not always easy, and scientists often face a range of problems that can impede their progress. In the following pages, we will explore some of the most common problems that scientists encounter and suggest some ways to address them.

As we have already experienced in other parts of our lives, one of the most significant challenges that scientists face is securing funding for their research. Research projects require significant resources, including personnel, equipment, and supplies. However, funding sources for research are often limited, and competition for grants can be fierce. Scientists may need to spend considerable time writing grant proposals, networking with potential funders, and justifying the value of their research.

I would like to highlight that scientific research is a time-consuming process that requires patience and dedication. However, scientists also have other responsibilities, such as teaching, writing, and administrative duties. Balancing these different roles can be difficult, and many scientists struggle to find enough time to devote to their research projects. Time management skills, such as prioritization and delegation, can be essential in helping scientists make the most of their available time.

Another aspect we should keep in mind is that science is often a collaborative endeavor, with researchers working together on large-scale projects. However, collaboration can also be challenging, particularly when working with colleagues from different disciplines or with different communication styles. Communication skills, such as active listening, clear writing, and diplomatic language, can be critical in fostering effective collaboration.

We live in an era of excessive information and scientific research generates vast amounts of data, and managing this data can be a significant challenge. Data must be collected, stored, analyzed, and interpreted in a way that is transparent and reproducible. Data management skills, such as data organization, documentation, and archiving, can be essential in ensuring that scientific research is both rigorous and reliable.

Another important issue to consider is that scientific research must be conducted in an ethical and responsible manner. However, ethical considerations can be complex, and scientists must navigate a range of ethical issues, such as informed consent, animal welfare, and conflicts of interest. Ethical training and education can be essential in helping scientists navigate these issues and make informed decisions.

Finally, I would like to stress that science is a challenging and rewarding field, but it is not without its problems. Scientists must navigate a range of challenges, from securing funding to managing data to collaborating with colleagues. However, we should be confident and optimistic that by developing skills in time management, collaboration, data management, and ethics, scientists can overcome these challenges and make meaningful contributions to their field. And to that, I would add hard work, discipline, and persistence.

3 GENERAL STRATEGIES FOR SELF-IMPROVEMENT

Before elaborating on the good practices and tips for success in science, I would like to point out the value of building a positive mentality. Self-improvement is the process of enhancing one's skills, knowledge, and character traits. It is a continuous journey that requires commitment, dedication, and effort. The good news is that everyone can improve themselves if they are willing to put in the work. In this section, we will discuss various strategies for self-improvement that you can use to develop your skills and achieve your goals.

I would say that the first step towards self-improvement is setting clear and specific goals. You should know what you want to achieve and define your goals accordingly. Goals should be realistic, achievable, and measurable. It is essential to write down your goals and track your progress regularly.

Of course, a growth mindset is essential for self-improvement. It means that you believe that you can develop your abilities through hard work, dedication, and learning. Embrace challenges and see them as opportunities to learn and grow. Recognize that failures and mistakes are part of the learning process.

It is important to remember that reading is an excellent way to acquire new knowledge and expand your understanding of various topics. Read books, articles, and other materials related to your goals and interests. Attend seminars, workshops, and training sessions to learn from experts and gain new insights.

Let's keep in mind that self-discipline is a critical factor in self-improvement. It means that you have the ability to control your actions, emotions, and thoughts to achieve your goals. Practice self-discipline by setting routines, managing your time effectively, and avoiding distractions.

Feedback is crucial for self-improvement. It helps you identify areas of strength and weaknesses and provides guidance on how to improve. Seek feedback from friends, colleagues, and mentors who can provide constructive criticism and support.

I guess it seems obvious but developing good habits is an essential part of self-improvement. Good habits can help you stay focused, motivated, and productive. Examples of good habits include regular exercise, healthy eating, and getting enough sleep.

It is great to have positive thinking but self-improvement also requires taking action. It is not enough to have goals and knowledge; you must apply what you learn and take action to achieve your goals. Take small steps towards your goals every day, and you will see progress over time.

Let's all keep in mind that self-improvement is a lifelong journey that requires effort and dedication. I would dare to ensure you that by setting clear goals, cultivating a growth mindset, developing self-discipline, learning new skills, practicing self-care, surrounding yourself with positive influences, and practicing gratitude, you can achieve your goals and lead a fulfilling life. Remember that self-improvement is a process, and it is important to be patient and persistent in your efforts. We can try to compare our present with past skills and knowledge and identify weaknesses to be improved in the future.

4 USEFUL SKILLS FOR SCIENTISTS

We can be sure that being a scientist requires more than just a strong foundation in a particular scientific field. Scientists must also possess a diverse range of skills to effectively conduct research, communicate their findings, and collaborate with others. In the following pages, we will discuss some of the most important skills that scientists should develop to excel in their careers.

Let's start with critical thinking which is a crucial skill for scientists as it enables them to evaluate evidence, make logical deductions, and draw conclusions. Scientists must be able to analyze complex data, identify patterns, and make informed decisions based on their findings. Critical thinking involves asking questions, challenging assumptions, and considering alternative explanations, all of which are essential for scientific inquiry. Usually, education in schools and colleges emphasizes memorizing long texts rather than building critical thinking. On the other hand, working on projects and encouraging team work would greatly contribute to more creative thinking.

Effective communication is another essential skill for scientists. Scientists must be able to articulate their findings to a variety of audiences, including other scientists, policymakers, and the general public. Good communication skills include the ability to write clear and concise reports, present data in a compelling way, and explain technical concepts to non-experts. This is often the weakest point of many scientists. You may see the most brilliant researcher failing hard to present his work at a conference or discussing with a journalist during an interview. Actually, most scientists avoid communication with the press or large audiences. In a later chapter, we will discuss some improvement tips.

Collaboration is an important skill for scientists as research is often a team effort. Scientists must be able to work with others, share ideas, and contribute to a common goal. Good collaboration skills include the ability to listen actively, give and receive feedback, and resolve conflicts in a constructive manner. One person alone cannot go too far, while a group of people can achieve miracles.

Adaptability is an important skill for scientists as research can be unpredictable and often requires scientists to adjust their plans and approaches. Scientists must be able to think on their feet, make quick decisions, and adjust to changing circumstances. Good adaptability skills include being flexible, open-minded, and able to learn quickly. Let's take the example of a researcher. An experiment is an open question and one cannot predict the response of the treatment under investigation. Based on the early findings, the researcher should be able to adapt the plan and move to the next experimental step.

Time management is an essential skill for scientists as research can be time-consuming and often requires scientists to juggle multiple projects and deadlines. Scientists must be able to prioritize tasks, manage their time effectively, and meet deadlines. Good time management skills include the ability to plan ahead, set realistic goals, and use time efficiently. Failing to meet deadlines can be destructive for a scientist's career.

Technical skills are also important for scientists as they often work with complex equipment and software. Scientists must be able to operate and maintain laboratory equipment, use statistical software, and analyze data using a variety of techniques. Good technical skills include the ability to troubleshoot problems, stay up-to-date with new technologies, and seek out additional training when necessary. The good news is that a scientist can focus on the techniques that are relevant for a specific research field and master the use of specific equipment needed.

Creativity is an important skill for scientists as it enables them to generate new ideas, approaches, and solutions. Scientists must be able to think outside the box, take risks, and explore new avenues of research. Good creativity skills include the ability to brainstorm ideas, experiment with new methods, and take calculated risks. A habit that boosts creative thinking is to zoom out of work and get a broad knowledge of life. Furthermore, carefully observing things, people, and nature around us can be a great source of inspiration.

In summary, we could say that scientists must possess a wide range of skills to succeed in their careers. Critical thinking, communication, collaboration, adaptability, time management, technical skills, and creativity are all essential skills for scientists to develop. By cultivating these skills, scientists can improve their research, communicate their findings effectively, and contribute to scientific progress. Don't worry if you don't have all those skills yet, progress comes through time and persistent effort!

5 FINDING THE RIGHT MENTOR

Like all athletes have a coach, we could say that all scientists should have a mentor! A good mentor can provide guidance, support, and encouragement, and help you navigate the many challenges of a career in science. However, finding the right mentor can be a hard task, especially for early-career scientists. Let's explore some strategies for finding the right mentor in science.

I guess we would all agree that before you start looking for a mentor, it is essential to identify your goals and needs. What do you hope to achieve in your career? What skills do you need to develop? What challenges do you face? By understanding your goals and needs, you can find a mentor who can help you achieve them.

Of course, networking is an important way to find a mentor. Attend scientific conferences, seminars, and workshops in your field. Join professional organizations and attend their events. Connect with other scientists on social media platforms like LinkedIn and Twitter. By building a strong network, you can meet potential mentors and learn more about their research and mentoring style.

I suggest that when looking for a mentor, it is essential to find someone with experience. Look for mentors who have a track record of success in your field. Consider the mentor's research publications, grants, and awards. Also, look for mentors who have experience mentoring others, especially early-career scientists.

For the guidance procedure to succeed, it is essential to find a mentor with whom you are compatible. Consider the mentor's personality, communication style, and mentoring philosophy. Look for someone who can offer constructive feedback, support, and encouragement. Consider if the mentor has time and availability to invest in your mentorship. This is very important because the most successful scientists that we would like to have as mentors are probably too busy to devote enough time to consulting an early career researcher.

It is important to seek out mentors from diverse backgrounds and perspectives. Consider mentors from different genders, ethnicities, and cultures. Mentors with different backgrounds and perspectives can provide unique insights and help you develop a broad perspective on your research.

You could ask colleagues, professors, and other mentors for recommendations. They may know of someone who would be a good fit for you. Additionally, many institutions have formal mentoring programs that can help you connect with a mentor.

After preparation comes the action. Once you have identified potential mentors, it is essential to reach out to them. Write a professional and compelling email that explains who you are, your research interests, and why you are interested in their mentorship. Be specific about what you hope to achieve from the mentorship and how often you would like to meet.

Let's keep in mind that finding the right mentor is crucial for success in science. If we identify our goals and needs, network, seek out diversity, and ask for recommendations, we can find a mentor who can help us achieve our goals. Once you have identified potential mentors, it is essential to reach out to them professionally and explicitly. With the right mentorship, you can thrive in science and achieve your career goals. You may also consider having multiple mentors to ask for advice, something like an expert committee but in the end, you should process all the ideas and suggestions and take responsibility for decisions.

6 DEVELOP A CAREER PLAN

When we start an enterprise the first action is to prepare a business plan, right? Similarly, developing a career plan is a critical step for anyone looking to build a successful career in science. A career plan is a roadmap that helps individuals identify their career goals, skills, and interests, and develop a plan to achieve them. I will now present the steps involved in developing a career plan in science.

I cannot stress enough that the first step in developing a career plan is to conduct a self-assessment. This involves taking a critical look at your skills, interests, and values. Start by asking yourself the following questions:

What are my strengths and weaknesses?

What are my interests?

What values are important to me?

Once you have answered these questions, you can use the information to identify potential career paths that align with your skills, interests, and values.

After conducting a self-assessment, the next step is to research potential career paths in science. This involves gathering information about different career paths, such as job duties, required education and experience, and salary expectations. You can use resources like job boards, career websites, and industry associations to gather this information. Meeting in person and discussing with people of various professions is an excellent way to get relevant information.

I guess you would agree that based on your self-assessment and research, you should now have a better understanding of your career aspirations. The next step is to set specific career goals that align with your interests and values. Your goals should be SMART: Specific, Measurable, Achievable, Relevant, and Time-bound.

Once you have identified your career goals, the next step is to develop a plan to achieve them. This plan should include short-term and long-term goals, as well as actionable steps to achieve those goals. For example, if your goal is to become a research scientist, your plan may include earning a Ph.D., gaining research experience, and publishing papers in scientific journals.

I will repeat multiple times in this book that building a network is an essential part of developing a successful career in science. This involves connecting with other professionals in your field, attending conferences and networking events, and reaching out to potential mentors. A strong network can provide valuable support, advice, and career opportunities.

You may have already realized that science is a rapidly evolving field, and it is essential to continuously learn and develop new skills to stay relevant. This involves staying up-to-date with the latest research, attending training programs and workshops, and pursuing additional education or certifications.

In summary, let's remember that by conducting a self-assessment, researching career paths, setting career goals, developing a plan, building a network, and continuously learning and developing skills, we can achieve our career aspirations and make meaningful contributions to the scientific community. On the other hand, if we move without a plan, we may end up in a completely irrelevant condition in our lives compared to our initial ambitions, wondering "how did I get here?" Let's try to avoid that scenario!

7 BUILDING A STRONG PROFESSIONAL NETWORK

In my personal life, having friends and family are the ultimate success milestones. In a similar sense, in the field of science, building a strong professional network can be vital for career success. A professional network can help you find job opportunities, collaborate on research projects, gain new skills, and keep up-to-date with the latest developments in your field. In this chapter, I will present some strategies for building a strong professional network in science.

Definitely, conferences and events are a great way to meet new people in your field. Make sure to attend conferences that are relevant to your interests and research. During the early career stages of a scientist when funding is scarce, I would recommend selecting the single most specialized conference for your discipline and attending as more of its events as possible. When attending, take the time to introduce yourself to other attendees and engage in conversations. Attend presentations and ask questions during Q&A sessions. This will help you to establish yourself as a knowledgeable and engaged member of the scientific community.

In addition, joining professional organizations can provide access to a wealth of resources, including job postings, educational materials, and networking opportunities. Make sure to choose an organization that is relevant to your area of expertise and try to participate in their events and activities. Consider volunteering for a leadership position within the organization to expand your network and gain leadership experience. Some professional organizations have an expensive annual subscription that may be limiting to many scientists. In such a case, start with some relevant, free, or low-cost professional organizations.

I would also suggest that connecting with colleagues is a great way to build a strong professional network. Reach out to colleagues in your department or in related fields and ask to meet for coffee or lunch. Discuss your research interests and ask about their work. Stay in touch by regularly attending departmental events and seminars. Send emails about events or papers that may be of interest to a colleague.

Of course, social media platforms such as LinkedIn, Twitter, and ResearchGate are great tools for building a professional network. Make sure to keep your profiles up-to-date and engage with other users by commenting on their posts and sharing relevant content. Join groups and discussions related to your research interests to expand your network and stay up-to-date with the latest developments in your field. There is a risk of getting overinvolved in digital networking and spending excessive time on those platforms, so I recommend scheduling a specific time slot per day or week for this activity.

Collaborating on research projects with other scientists can help you to establish strong professional connections. Seek out researchers who are working on projects related to your research interests and propose a collaboration. This can lead to new research opportunities, publications, and presentations. Remember that successful project implementation will bring new project opportunities but a bad performance may leave you out of future initiatives, so do your best.

Workshops and training sessions can provide opportunities to learn new skills and connect with other professionals in your field. Look for workshops and training sessions that are relevant to your research interests and attend them. Take the opportunity to introduce yourself to other attendees and engage in discussions. There are more and more online courses that you can attend at low or no cost.

Keep in mind that building a strong professional network in science is crucial for career success. I suggest attending conferences and events, joining professional organizations, connecting with colleagues, using social media, collaborating on research projects, and attending workshops and training sessions to expand your network and stay up-to-date with the latest developments in your field. Remember to be proactive and engaged in your interactions with other professionals, and always be open to new opportunities for collaboration and connection. Also, please keep in mind that networking is based on human interaction, and human relationships are based on mutual respect.

8 SUCCESS TIPS FOR SCIENTISTS

In a few words, we will present here some tips to improve our efficiency in science. We will elaborate on them in later chapters. Some concepts are intentionally repeated in several chapters of this book to emphasize their importance and to provide various points of view.

- Set clear goals: Having clear, achievable goals can help you stay focused and motivated in your scientific work.

- Develop a strong work ethic: Science often requires long hours, persistence, and attention to detail. Developing a strong work ethic can help you achieve success in the field.

- Collaborate with others: Collaboration with other scientists can help you access new ideas, techniques, and data that you may not have access to on your own.

- Communicate your findings: Communication is a crucial part of science. Effective communication skills can help you share your findings with other scientists, as well as with the public.

- Stay up-to-date with the latest developments: Science is constantly evolving, so it's important to stay up-to-date with the latest developments in your field.

- Take calculated risks: Science often involves taking calculated risks to explore new ideas and techniques. Don't be afraid to try something new, but always be thoughtful and careful in your approach.

- Be open-minded and curious: Curiosity and open-mindedness are essential traits for any scientist. A willingness to explore new ideas and approaches can lead to breakthrough discoveries.

- Embrace failure: Science involves a lot of trial and error. Don't be discouraged by failure; instead, use it as an opportunity to learn and grow.

- Be patient: Scientific breakthroughs often take time. Be patient and persistent in your work, and don't give up on your goals.

- Seek out mentorship: Finding a mentor who can offer guidance and support can be invaluable in the field of science. Look for opportunities to connect with experienced scientists who can offer insights and advice.

9 A DAY IN THE WORK OF A RESEARCHER

I have been working as a researcher in Greece for almost two decades now and I must confess that I love my job! By the way, Greece is a beautiful country in Southeastern Europe worth visiting. But let's get back to the point. As a researcher, each day is unique and filled with surprises. The work is never boring, and there is always something new to discover. A typical day begins early in the morning, as the researchers arrive at their lab or office, ready to dive into their work. The first task of the day is usually to catch up on emails and correspondence. Researchers often receive a large number of emails each day, ranging from inquiries about their work to requests for collaboration. Responding to these emails is an important part of the job, as it helps to maintain connections with colleagues and keep abreast of new developments in the field. Keep in mind that failing to reply to some messages promptly may result in losing a great opportunity for collaboration.

After responding to emails, the researcher will typically spend some time reviewing the literature. This involves reading through scientific papers and other publications relevant to their area of research. This helps the researcher stay up to date on the latest findings and ensures that their work is grounded in the most current knowledge. Once the researcher has reviewed the literature, they will typically begin working on their research projects. This could involve conducting experiments in a lab, analyzing data, or writing up findings for publication. Depending on the nature of the research, this work may be done alone or in collaboration with other researchers. Establishing a lab group and efficiently coordinating it is of paramount importance for the success of a researcher. As said earlier, one person cannot go too far alone but a group of well-going people can achieve miracles! Meticulously select your associates by examining their CVs and recommendations, and their relevance to your research field. Of course, these features are not enough. The necessary element for a collaboration to succeed is to have communication compatibility with your associates. Some people get along well and get harmonized with a few words and others are simply not for each other like they are speaking different languages. Don't force to make two incompatible persons match. Instead, you are advised to emphasize multiple interviews and a trial period before signing a contract with a new group member.

One of the most exciting aspects of being a researcher is the opportunity to discover something new. This could be a new finding in a lab experiment or a novel interpretation of existing data. The thrill of discovery is what drives many researchers to pursue their work, and it can be incredibly satisfying to see the results of months or even years of effort come to fruition. Sometimes, in our rush to run a lot of experiments and publish papers fast, we don't devote enough time to identify real-life problems that we should solve or stakeholders' needs we should try to fulfill through our research. These two points should be our priorities at all times.

Throughout the day, researchers may also attend meetings or give presentations. These can be with colleagues within their department, or they may involve external collaborators or stakeholders. These meetings are an important way to share ideas and discuss progress on ongoing research projects.

It is sad to say that much of the time of a researcher is wasted on red-tape work, preparing unimportant documents and unnecessary reports for administration procedures. If you could hire an assistant to do all this paperwork you will save a lot of time to invest in really productive activities such as running experiments and writing papers and grants.

As the day draws to a close, the researcher will typically spend some time organizing their notes and preparing for the next day. This could involve updating lab notebooks, reviewing data, or making plans for upcoming experiments. Researchers often work long hours and have a lot on their plates, so being organized and efficient is essential for success in the field. A good idea is to plan the activities of the following day for you and your group and each day monitor the progress achieved.

I must say that the life of a researcher is a busy and exciting one. Each day brings new challenges and opportunities for discovery, and the work is never boring. Whether conducting experiments, analyzing data, or collaborating with colleagues, researchers play an important role in advancing our understanding of the world around us. And the bonus of the work of a researcher is the opportunity to travel to different countries for international collaboration projects and this way have the chance to see beautiful places and meet interesting people. What more to ask for?

10 SUCCESS IN JOB APPLICATION IN RESEARCH CENTERS

Success in job applications for research centers can be achieved by following some key steps.

Research the research center: It is important to research the research center before applying for a position to understand its research goals and focus areas. This will help you tailor your application to showcase how your skills and experience align with the center's research goals.

Customize your application: Tailor your application to the specific job posting and research center you are applying to. Make sure your application highlights how your skills and experience are relevant to the position and research center.

Showcase your skills and experience: Highlight your skills and experience that are relevant to the job position and research center. Use specific examples of how you have applied your skills and experience in previous roles and how they can contribute to the research center's goals.

Network with people in the industry: Networking with people in the industry can provide valuable insights into the research center and its hiring process. It can also lead to potential job opportunities and referrals.

Follow up: After submitting your application, follow up with the research center to express your continued interest in the position and inquire about the status of your application.

Be prepared for an interview: If selected for an interview, prepare well by researching the research center and the interviewers, and practice your responses to common interview questions. Be ready to demonstrate your knowledge of the research center's work and how you can contribute to its goals.

11 PREPARE YOUR CV FOR A RESEARCH CENTER

Name:
Contact Information:

Email: [insert email address]
Phone: [insert phone number]
Education:

PhD in [field of study], [university], [year of graduation]
Master's Degree in [field of study], [university], [year of graduation]
Bachelor's Degree in [field of study], [university], [year of graduation]
Research Experience:

[Current Position], [Current Institution], [start date-present]
Responsibilities: [list of responsibilities and duties]
[Previous Position], [Previous Institution], [start date-end date]
Responsibilities: [list of responsibilities and duties]
Skills:

Proficient in [list of programming languages or software tools]
Experienced in [list of research methods or techniques]
Strong written and verbal communication skills
Ability to work independently and in a team environment
Excellent problem-solving and critical thinking skills
Publications:

[List of publications, including journal articles, conference papers, and

book chapters]
    Professional Memberships:

    [List of professional organizations and societies]
    References:

    [List of three references with their contact information]

12 THE WORK OF A UNIVERSITY PROFESSOR

If you interview a thousand scientists, probably the vast majority will say that their dream job is to become a university professor. A university professor is a highly respected and desired position in academia. They are responsible for educating the next generation of leaders and making significant contributions to their field of study. This chapter will explore the work of university professors, including their responsibilities, daily tasks, and qualifications required to excel in this profession.

As you may imagine, a university professor has many responsibilities, including teaching, research, and service. Teaching involves preparing and delivering lectures, grading assignments, and working with students to ensure their academic success. Research involves conducting original research, publishing papers, and presenting findings at conferences. Service involves serving on committees, mentoring students, and engaging in outreach activities.

A typical day for a university professor can vary widely depending on their department, tenure status, and level of seniority. However, most professors spend a significant amount of time preparing lectures, meeting with students, and conducting research. They may also attend committee meetings, collaborate with colleagues, and engage in outreach activities. Do you like interacting with a lot of people all day? Can you tolerate multiple unplanned meetings with students? These are two important points to consider for deciding whether this profession is good for you.

We should keep in mind that to become a university professor, one must typically hold a doctoral degree in their field of study. In addition, they must have a strong record of scholarly achievement, including publications, presentations, and grants. Teaching experience is also important, as is a commitment to service and engagement in their academic community. Finally, many universities require professors to obtain tenure, which involves a rigorous review process to ensure that they have made significant contributions to their field of study.

Despite the many rewards of being a university professor, there are also many challenges. One of the biggest challenges is the pressure to publish scientific articles, which can be time-consuming and stressful. In addition, tenure can be difficult to obtain, and many professors experience job insecurity until they are granted tenure. Finally, balancing teaching, research, and service can be challenging, and many professors struggle to find the right balance.

In summary, I would say that being a university professor is a rewarding but challenging profession. Professors are responsible for educating the next generation of leaders and making significant contributions to their field of study. They spend their days preparing lectures, conducting research, and engaging in service activities. To become a university professor, one must hold a doctoral degree, have a strong record of scholarly achievement, and commit to teaching, research, and service. Last but not least, strong communication skills are necessary to be able to transfer knowledge to the students. While there are many challenges to this profession, the rewards are significant, and many professors find great fulfillment in their work. As with any educational profession, some people have the teacher talent and require minimum effort to function in a classroom while others strangle to lecture and might have a hard time being university professors.

13 SUCCESS IN JOB APPLICATION IN UNIVERSITIES

Success in job applications in universities can depend on a variety of factors, including your qualifications, experience, networking, and the competitiveness of the position. Here are some tips to increase your chances of success.

Ensure that your application materials (resume, cover letter, teaching, and research statements) are customized to the specific position and university you are applying to. Highlight your relevant experience, skills, and qualifications.

Attend academic conferences and events to meet faculty and administrators at universities where you are interested in working. This can help you learn more about the university, its culture, and the types of positions that are available.

Before applying, research the university and the department you are applying to. Look for information on their mission, culture, values, and current faculty research.

Universities typically prioritize candidates who have a strong record of teaching and research. Make sure to emphasize your experience in these areas in your application materials.

Build your CV by publishing articles, presenting at conferences, and participating in research projects. The more experience you have in your field, the better your chances of securing a position in a university.

If you are invited to an interview, make sure to prepare thoroughly. Research the university and the department, and practice answering common interview questions.

After submitting your application, follow up with the hiring manager to express your continued interest in the position. This can help keep your application top of mind and demonstrate your enthusiasm for the opportunity.

Remember, the academic job market can be competitive, so it's important to be persistent and patient. Keep applying and building your experience, and you will increase your chances of success in job applications at universities. Building expertise in a topic that has low competition in the academic community would certainly make your life easier.

14 PREPARE YOUR CV FOR A UNIVERSITY

[Full Name]
[Address]
[Phone Number]
[Email Address]

Objective:
To obtain a challenging position as a [position] at [University Name] where I can utilize my [skills] and [experience] to contribute to the academic community and advance my career.

Education:

[Degree], [Major], [University Name], [Graduation Date]
[Degree], [Major], [University Name], [Graduation Date]
[Degree], [Major], [University Name], [Graduation Date]
Experience:

[Job Title], [Company Name], [Employment Dates]

[Responsibility 1]
[Responsibility 2]
[Responsibility 3]
[Job Title], [Company Name], [Employment Dates]

[Responsibility 1]
[Responsibility 2]
[Responsibility 3]
Skills:

[Skill 1]
[Skill 2]
[Skill 3]
[Skill 4]
[Skill 5]
Publications:

[Publication 1]
[Publication 2]
[Publication 3]
Awards and Honors:

[Award/Honor 1]
[Award/Honor 2]
[Award/Honor 3]
Professional Memberships:

[Membership 1]
[Membership 2]
[Membership 3]
References:
Available upon request.

15 WORKING AS A SCIENTIST FOR AN INDUSTRY

Being a scientist does not necessarily mean having a career in a university or a research center. Working as a scientist for an industry can be a rewarding and exciting career choice for individuals with a strong background in science and a passion for applying their knowledge to real-world problems. In this chapter, I will share with you the unique aspects of working as a scientist for industry, including the different types of industries that employ scientists, the roles and responsibilities of a scientist in industry, and the skills required for success in this field.

It is great news that scientists are employed in a variety of industries, including pharmaceuticals, biotechnology, healthcare, environmental sciences, food and beverage, energy, and technology. Each industry has its unique demands and requirements for scientists. For instance, in the pharmaceutical industry, scientists are involved in the development and testing of new drugs. In contrast, scientists in the food and beverage industry work on the development and improvement of food products.

As you can expect, the roles and responsibilities of a scientist in an industry can vary depending on the industry and the specific job function. However, some common responsibilities of a scientist in the industry include:

- Conducting research and development activities to improve existing products or develop new ones
- Designing and conducting experiments to test the effectiveness and safety of new products
- Analyzing data and preparing reports to communicate research findings to other team members or stakeholders
- Collaborating with other scientists, engineers, and product development teams to ensure that products meet the needs of the

market and comply with regulatory requirements
- Keeping up to date with the latest developments in their field and incorporating new knowledge into their work.

It is important to remember that working as a scientist in the industry requires a combination of scientific knowledge, technical skills, and soft skills. Some of the critical skills required for success in this field include:
- Strong analytical and problem-solving skills
- Excellent written and verbal communication skills
- The ability to work collaboratively in a team environment
- Attention to detail and accuracy in data analysis
- Knowledge of regulatory requirements and compliance standards
- The ability to manage multiple projects and priorities simultaneously.

Working as a scientist in an industry can be challenging, and it is essential to be aware of these challenges. Some of the significant challenges include:
- Balancing the need for scientific rigor with the demands of a fast-paced industry environment
- Navigating complex regulatory frameworks and compliance standards
- Working within budget constraints and meeting tight deadlines
- Communicating complex scientific findings to non-scientific stakeholders.

Let's keep in mind that working as a scientist in the industry can be a fulfilling and exciting career choice for individuals with a passion for science and a desire to apply their knowledge to real-world problems. The role of a scientist in the industry can vary depending on the industry and job function, but common responsibilities include research and development, data analysis, and collaboration with other team members. The skills required for success in this field include scientific knowledge, technical skills, and soft skills such as communication and collaboration. Ending this chapter, I guess we would all agree that while there are challenges associated with working in the industry, the opportunity to make a meaningful impact in the world of science and industry can be incredibly rewarding.

16 SUCCESS IN JOB APPLICATION IN THE INDUSTRY

To increase your chances of success in a job application in the industry, there are several steps you can take.

Tailor your resume and cover letter to the specific job and industry. Use keywords and phrases from the job description to show that you have the necessary skills and experience.

Attend industry events, join professional organizations, and connect with people on LinkedIn. This can help you learn more about the industry and job opportunities, as well as make valuable connections.

Learn about the company's mission, values, and products or services. Understand the industry trends and challenges, and how the company fits into the industry.

Research common interview questions and practice your responses. Be ready to discuss your skills and experience and how they relate to the job and the company.

Send a thank-you note or email to the interviewer, and reiterate your interest in the job. This can help keep you on top of their mind and show that you are serious about the opportunity.

Job searching can be a long and difficult process, but it's important to stay positive and keep working towards your goal. Keep applying to jobs, networking, and refining your skills and experience. Eventually, the right opportunity will come along.

17 PREPARE YOUR CV FOR AN INDUSTRY

[Full Name]
[Address]
[Phone Number]
[Email Address]

Objective:
To obtain a challenging position in [Industry] utilizing my skills and experience.

Education:
[Degree], [Major], [Institution], [Graduation Date]
[Degree], [Major], [Institution], [Graduation Date]

Skills:

[Skill 1]
[Skill 2]
[Skill 3]
[Skill 4]
[Skill 5]
Experience:

[Job Title], [Company Name], [Employment Dates]

[Job Duty 1]
[Job Duty 2]
[Job Duty 3]
[Job Duty 4]

[Job Duty 5]
[Job Title], [Company Name], [Employment Dates]

[Job Duty 1]
[Job Duty 2]
[Job Duty 3]
[Job Duty 4]
[Job Duty 5]
Certifications:

[Certification 1], [Issuing Organization], [Date]
[Certification 2], [Issuing Organization], [Date]
References:
Available upon request.

18 WORKING AS A LAB ANALYST

I remember when we were kids, in all cartoons and movies a scientist was depicted in a laboratory wearing a white coat and holding vessels with bubbling liquids of all colors of the rainbow! Even in our days, there are many board games for children named something like "the young scientist" and provide some basic tools for simple experiments. My sons loved mixing powders with liquids and observing some color changes or smoke coming out of the test tube! This could be fun also for adults, so why not? Working as a lab analyst can be a challenging and rewarding career choice. Lab analysts play a crucial role in the scientific community by conducting experiments, analyzing data, and providing accurate and reliable results. In the following pages, we will explore the day-to-day responsibilities of a lab analyst, the necessary skills and qualifications, and the potential career paths available.

As expected, the primary responsibility of a lab analyst is to conduct experiments and analyze data. This requires a high level of attention to detail and a methodical approach. Lab analysts must also be able to troubleshoot problems that arise during experiments and adjust protocols as necessary. They are responsible for maintaining accurate records and keeping up-to-date with new research in their field.

In addition to conducting experiments, lab analysts must also ensure that the laboratory is well-maintained and that all equipment is functioning properly. They are responsible for ordering supplies and keeping an inventory of reagents and other materials. Lab analysts also play a role in training new staff members and mentoring students.

A bachelor's degree in a scientific discipline is typically required to work as a lab analyst. Degrees in chemistry, biology, or biochemistry are common, but other disciplines may also be relevant depending on the specific field. Lab analysts must also have a solid understanding of laboratory techniques, data analysis, and statistical methods.

In addition to formal education, lab analysts must also possess excellent communication skills, both written and verbal. They must be able to work collaboratively with other team members, including scientists, technicians, and administrative staff. Attention to detail and a strong work ethic are also essential traits for a successful lab analyst.

It is good news that working as a lab analyst can lead to a variety of career paths. Some lab analysts may choose to pursue advanced degrees in their field, such as a master's or Ph.D. This can lead to opportunities for more senior positions, such as laboratory manager or research scientist.

On the other hand, some other lab analysts may choose to specialize in a particular area, such as forensic science or environmental testing. Specialization can lead to opportunities for higher pay and increased job security. Lab analysts may also choose to work in a variety of settings, such as government agencies, academic research labs, or private industry.

Closing this chapter, I would like to mention that working as a lab analyst requires a combination of technical knowledge, attention to detail, and strong communication skills. While the job can be challenging at times, it is also highly rewarding. Lab analysts play a vital role in advancing scientific research and improving our understanding of the world around us. I dare to ensure you that with the right qualifications and dedication, a career as a lab analyst can lead to a lifetime of fulfilling work. And as mentioned at the beginning of this chapter, this profession may fulfill our childhood dreams!

19 HEALTH AND SAFETY IN LABORATORIES

Ok, working in a lab sounds fun but it's not exactly a playground! Laboratories are environments where scientific experiments and research are conducted. They may include chemical, biological, and physical hazards that can pose a risk to the health and safety of laboratory workers. It is, therefore, crucial to implement health and safety measures to ensure that laboratory workers are protected from potential hazards. This chapter discusses the health and safety measures that should be implemented in laboratories.

Hazard Identification
The first step in ensuring laboratory safety is to identify potential hazards. Hazard identification involves identifying potential hazards in the laboratory, including chemical, biological, and physical hazards. This process requires a thorough assessment of the laboratory, including the type of experiments conducted and the equipment used. Once potential hazards have been identified, appropriate safety measures can be implemented.

Chemical Safety
Chemicals are commonly used in laboratories, and they can pose a risk to the health and safety of laboratory workers. Chemical safety measures include using appropriate personal protective equipment (PPE), such as gloves, goggles, and lab coats. Chemicals should also be stored in appropriate containers and labeled correctly. In addition, it is essential to have a chemical spill response plan in place in case of an accident.

Biological Safety
Biological hazards, such as bacteria and viruses, can also pose a risk to laboratory workers. Biological safety measures include using appropriate PPE, such as gloves, goggles, and lab coats. In addition, all biological waste

should be disposed of appropriately, and laboratories that work with hazardous biological agents should follow appropriate guidelines and regulations.

Physical Safety

Physical hazards in laboratories include electrical hazards, radiation hazards, and fire hazards. Safety measures for physical hazards include following appropriate procedures for handling electrical equipment, such as using circuit breakers and wearing appropriate PPE. Radiation hazards should be handled by trained professionals, and fire safety measures include having fire extinguishers and smoke detectors in the laboratory.

Emergency Response

Emergency response plans should be in place in case of accidents or incidents in the laboratory. This includes having appropriate equipment on hand, such as fire extinguishers and first aid kits. It is also essential to have clear procedures for reporting incidents and evacuating the laboratory in case of an emergency.

Training and Education

All laboratory workers should receive appropriate training and education on laboratory safety. This includes training on the safe handling of chemicals, biological agents, and physical hazards. In addition, all laboratory workers should be aware of emergency procedures and how to report incidents.

Ending this chapter I would like to highlight that laboratory safety is crucial for protecting the health and safety of laboratory workers. It is essential to identify potential hazards and implement appropriate safety measures, including chemical safety, biological safety, physical safety, emergency response, and training and education. If we all pay attention to these measures, we can ensure that laboratory workers can work safely and effectively in the laboratory environment.

20 CHECK OUT THESE WEBSITES WITH USEFUL INFORMATION AND CV TEMPLATES

Novoresume - This website offers a variety of templates for CVs and a step-by-step guide to help you create the perfect one.

Canva – Canva offers a range of customizable templates for CVs, making it incredibly easy to create a professional-looking CV.

VisualCV - This website is popular for its visual resume templates to create an eye-catching resume or CV.

Zety - Zety has easy-to-use online software which lets you create professional-looking CVs.

ResumeHelp – This website provides a good selection of editable CV templates with examples for all job categories.

MyPerfectResume - MyPerfectResume offers professional CV builders that help you create customized CVs as per your needs.

Resume.io – the website's templates are customizable, easy to use and the site allows you to create and collaborate with others.

Indeed – This website has a CV builder tool which helps you craft a professional CV that'll stand out from the competition

Hloom - This website provides excellent free downloadable CV templates that you can customize as per your needs.

Resume.com - This website allows you to create a CV easily and covers all the significant aspects of a professional and polished CV.

21 STARTING A BUSINESS IN SCIENCE

Some people don't feel well working for a boss and prefer to have independence and complete control of their job. I guess we would all agree that starting a science business can be a challenging and rewarding experience. There are many different paths that one can take when starting a business in this field, and each one requires careful planning and preparation. I will try to help you explore some of the key considerations that should be taken into account when starting a science business.

The first step in starting a science business is to identify a need in the marketplace. This could be a need for a new product or service, or it could be a need for a better solution to an existing problem. To identify a need, it is important to conduct thorough research and analysis of the market and potential customers. This may involve speaking with industry experts, conducting surveys, and analyzing industry reports and trends.

Once a need has been identified, the next step is to develop a business plan. A business plan should outline the key objectives of the business, the target market, the competitive landscape, the marketing strategy, and the financial projections. It is important to have a well-thought-out business plan to attract investors and to ensure that the business is set up for success.

Securing funding is a critical component of starting a science business. There are a variety of funding sources available, including venture capital, angel investors, and government grants. It is important to research the various options and to create a compelling pitch that demonstrates the potential of the business.

Building a strong team is essential for the success of any business. This includes finding talented individuals with relevant experience and expertise, as well as developing a strong company culture. It is important to create a collaborative and supportive environment that encourages innovation and creativity.

Intellectual property protection is critical for businesses in science. This may involve securing patents, trademarks, and copyrights, as well as developing confidentiality agreements and non-disclosure agreements. It is important to work with a qualified intellectual property attorney to ensure that all aspects of the business are properly protected.

Once all of the necessary groundwork has been laid, it is time to launch the business. This may involve developing a marketing strategy, building a website, and creating promotional materials. It is important to have a clear and compelling message that resonates with potential customers and investors.

As the business grows and expands, it will be important to develop strategies for scaling. This may involve expanding into new markets, developing new products and services, or partnering with other companies. It is important to remain agile and adaptable in order to take advantage of new opportunities as they arise.

I would like to highlight that if you want to start a science business, keep in mind that this is a challenging and rewarding experience. It requires careful planning, strategic thinking, and a strong team. If you take into consideration the tips outlined in this chapter, as entrepreneurs you can increase your chances of success and achieve your goals in the competitive world of science-based business. Who knows, maybe you will be the new Elon Musk of your generation!

22 EFFECTIVE TEAMWORK

University degrees and long CVs are great but some soft skills are also amazingly important. Effective teamwork is the process of collaborating with others to achieve a common goal. It requires individuals to work together, communicate effectively, and leverage each other's strengths to create a cohesive unit that is capable of accomplishing more than the sum of its parts. I will provide here some key principles to keep in mind for effective teamwork.

Communication is essential for successful teamwork. Members of the team need to be able to express themselves clearly and listen actively to each other.

Trust is fundamental to effective teamwork. Members need to feel that they can rely on each other to follow through on commitments, be honest and transparent, and work towards common goals.

Collaborating means working together to achieve a shared goal. Team members need to be willing to share information, ideas, and resources, and to work together to find solutions to challenges.

Diversity in the team can bring different perspectives and experiences, which can lead to more innovative ideas and better outcomes.

Each team member must be accountable for their actions and responsibilities. This means taking ownership of tasks and following through on commitments.

Teams need to be adaptable to changing circumstances and be willing to adjust their approach when necessary. This requires being open to feedback and new ideas and being willing to learn and grow.

Summarizing this chapter, I would like to mention that by following these principles, teams can develop a strong sense of unity, trust, and shared purpose, leading to more effective collaboration and better outcomes. Let's keep in mind that we are not robots. The human factor is always present in our work environment. We all have bad days, sensitivities, character peculiarities, and preferences for some tasks over others and it is a really challenging job to harmonize all these elements and make a team work efficiently.

23 HOW TO GET A PROMOTION AT WORK?

Is anybody interested in getting a promotion at work? Ok, I imagine most of us! Getting a promotion at work is often a result of a combination of factors, including your performance, attitude, and the company's needs. Here are some steps you can take to increase your chances of getting a promotion.

Let's start by making sure you have a clear understanding of your job description and the tasks and responsibilities that come with your role. This will help you identify areas where you can excel and demonstrate your value to the company.

You are advised to set clear and measurable goals for yourself that align with the company's objectives. Make sure to discuss these goals with your supervisor to ensure that you are on the right track.

Keep in mind to continuously improve your skills and knowledge through training, workshops, or further education. This will not only make you a more valuable employee but also demonstrate your commitment to your job and the company.

It is always a good strategy to take initiative and go above and beyond your job description by taking on additional responsibilities or projects that benefit the company.

It is important to build strong relationships with your coworkers and superiors. This can help you gain their support and advocacy when it comes time for a promotion.

Remember to seek regular feedback from your supervisor to understand areas where you can improve and demonstrate your willingness to learn and grow.

Of course, it is necessary to make it known to your supervisor that you are interested in getting a promotion and discuss what steps you need to take to make it happen. This can also help you understand what the company is looking for in a candidate for the position.

It may sound obvious, but please remember, promotions are not always guaranteed, but by taking these steps, you can position yourself as a strong candidate for advancement within your company. If you ask for what you want you may get it. If you don't, it is rather unlikely that your boss will start offering promotions and bonuses. But first, ask yourself these questions: how easy it is for my boss to replace me with another employee? How unique my role is?

24 TIPS FOR SUCCESS IN WORK LEADERSHIP

It is very prestigious for someone to be the CEO, the president, or the director of a company, a university, or a research center. Leadership is an essential component of any workplace, regardless of the industry or size of the organization. A leader's role is to guide and inspire their team members to achieve a common goal, while also fostering a positive work culture and empowering individuals to grow professionally. Effective leadership can make a significant impact on an organization's success, while poor leadership can lead to employee disengagement, high turnover rates, and a negative workplace environment. Let's see here the characteristics of effective leaders, the different types of leadership styles, and the importance of leadership in the workplace.

It is important to note that effective leaders possess a variety of characteristics that enable them to guide their team members successfully. Some of the key traits of effective leaders include:

Visionary: Effective leaders have a clear vision of where they want their organization to go and are able to communicate that vision to their team members.

Empathetic: Effective leaders understand their team members' perspectives and can relate to them on a personal level.

Communicative: Effective leaders are skilled communicators who are able to convey their ideas and instructions clearly and effectively.

Strategic Thinkers: Effective leaders can think strategically and make decisions that align with their organization's goals and values.

Authentic: Effective leaders are authentic to themselves, which helps to build trust and credibility with their team members.

Also, we should consider that there are many different types of leadership styles, each with its own strengths and weaknesses. Some of the most common leadership styles include:

Autocratic Leadership: In an autocratic leadership style, the leader makes all the decisions and expects team members to follow their instructions without question.

Transformational Leadership: Transformational leaders inspire and motivate their team members to achieve their goals by providing them with a sense of purpose and direction.

Servant Leadership: Servant leaders prioritize the needs of their team members above their own needs, working to create a positive work culture and empower individuals to grow professionally.

Democratic Leadership: In a democratic leadership style, the leader encourages team members to participate in the decision-making process and values their input.

Laissez-faire Leadership: In a laissez-faire leadership style, the leader takes a hands-off approach and allows team members to make their own decisions.

Let's remember that effective leadership is critical for a positive workplace environment and organizational success. When employees feel valued, supported, and empowered by their leaders, they are more likely to be engaged and committed to their work. Effective leaders can also help to foster a sense of collaboration and teamwork among their team members, which can lead to increased productivity and innovation.

On the other hand, poor leadership can have a detrimental impact on an organization. When leaders are uncommunicative, unresponsive, or lacking in empathy, employees may feel disengaged and unsupported, which can lead to high turnover rates and negative work culture.

At the end of this chapter, we could keep in mind that leadership is an essential component of any workplace, and effective leaders can have a significant impact on an organization's success. If we try possessing the right characteristics, using the right leadership style, and prioritizing the needs of our team members, we as leaders can create a positive work culture, foster collaboration and innovation, and empower individuals to grow professionally. It is very different to be a leader from being a boss!

25 HOW TO GET A RAISE AT WORK?

It seems to be in human nature to always aim higher. A better position at work, a better salary. Asking for a raise can be intimidating, but if you've been working hard and delivering good results, it's only fair to request a pay increase. The tricky part here is that the employees feel that they deserve a better salary based on their performance and the bosses think that they pay too much for the outcomes they get. Here are some steps you can take to increase your chances of getting a raise:

Do your research
Before asking for a raise, research the market value of your role in your industry and location. This can help you determine what your salary range should be.

Prepare your case
Make a list of your accomplishments, responsibilities, and contributions to the company. Highlight specific achievements and projects you've worked on that have benefited the company.

Schedule a meeting with your manager
Ask your manager for a meeting to discuss your performance and compensation. Be clear that you want to discuss a raise.

Make your case
During the meeting, present your accomplishments and contributions and explain why you believe you deserve a raise. Use data and metrics to support your case.

Be flexible

Be prepared to negotiate and consider other forms of compensation besides salary, such as bonuses, stock options, or additional benefits.

Follow up
If your manager needs time to consider your request, ask for a specific date when you can follow up. Be professional and respectful, even if your request is denied.

We should keep in mind that getting a raise is not guaranteed, but being prepared and presenting a strong case can increase your chances of success. Convince your boss that you offer much more than what you are paid for and that it would be hard to replace you and then a salary raise is more than possible. Remember that you may be considered the employee of the year by your boss when you are paid an X amount but you would probably be a bad deal for him if you are paid the double salary. So when asking for a raise, be prepared to receive increased expectations in work outcomes.

26 MAKE MONEY AND MANAGE IT EFFICIENTLY

Does this sound interesting? Money management is an essential skill that everyone should possess. Most people are not satisfied with their economic situation and many others make money and soon lose it because of terrible management. Whether you are earning a large salary or a modest one, knowing how to manage your money effectively can help you achieve your financial goals and lead a stress-free life. In the following paragraphs, I will provide you with some essential tips and strategies to help you manage your money more efficiently.

Budgeting
Please remember that the first step in effective money management is creating a budget. A budget is a financial plan that helps you track your income and expenses. It helps you to see where your money is going and identify areas where you can make savings. Creating a budget involves listing all your sources of income and all your expenses, including fixed expenses such as rent or mortgage payments, utility bills, and insurance, and variable expenses such as groceries, entertainment, and clothing. Once you have a clear picture of your income and expenses, you can set realistic financial goals and make adjustments to your spending habits to meet those goals.

Savings
I cannot stress enough that saving money is an essential part of money management. You should aim to save at least 10% of your income each month. One way to do this is to set up a separate savings account and transfer a fixed amount each month. You should also make use of any employer-sponsored retirement plans, and there are many available. Saving for

retirement should be a top priority, and starting early can help you achieve your financial goals more quickly.

Debt Management

I would like to highlight that managing your debt is another important aspect of money management. High-interest debt, such as credit card debt, can quickly spiral out of control and become a significant burden on your finances. One strategy for managing debt is to focus on paying off high-interest debt first, while making the minimum payments on other debts. Another approach is to consolidate your debt into a single loan with a lower interest rate. This can help you save money on interest payments and make it easier to manage your debt.

Investing

Most people are not familiar with this one, but investing your money can be an effective way to grow your wealth over time. Investing can help you achieve long-term financial goals, such as saving for retirement or buying a home. However, investing also carries some risks, and it is essential to understand those risks before investing. You should consult with a financial advisor to help you choose the right investment options and manage your portfolio.

Emergency Fund

Finally, it is important to have an emergency fund in place. An emergency fund is a sum of money set aside to cover unexpected expenses such as medical bills, car repairs, or job loss. Ideally, you should aim to have three to six months' worth of living expenses saved in your emergency fund. This can help you avoid taking on debt to cover unexpected expenses and provide peace of mind in case of a financial crisis.

I guess that you will all agree that effective money management is an essential skill that can help you achieve your financial goals and lead a stress-free life. If we organize our lives by creating a budget, saving money, managing our debt, investing wisely, and having an emergency fund in place, we can take control of our finances and build a secure financial future. Let's remember that with discipline, determination, and a little bit of planning, we can manage our money effectively and achieve financial freedom. It is not always the most important aspect of economic success how much you earn but how well you manage it.

27 HOW TO DESIGN AN EXPERIMENT?

The most fundamental activity of scientists is to perform experiments. However, many times experiments are not designed properly or an experimental design is totally absent. Designing an experiment involves several steps that are essential to ensure the validity and reliability of the results. Here is a general framework for designing an experiment.

Define the research question: Start by defining a clear research question that you want to answer through your experiment. This will guide your experimental design and help you identify the variables you need to manipulate and measure.

Identify the variables: Identify the independent variable(s) (the variable(s) you will manipulate) and dependent variable(s) (the variable(s) you will measure). Also, consider any extraneous variables that might affect your results and how you will control them.

Formulate a hypothesis: Based on your research question, formulate a hypothesis that predicts how the independent variable(s) will affect the dependent variable(s).

Choose a study design: Choose the type of study design that is appropriate for your research question and hypothesis. Common study designs include randomized controlled trials, quasi-experiments, and observational studies.

Determine the sample size: Determine the sample size needed to achieve adequate statistical power to test your hypothesis. Consider factors such as effect size, alpha level, and power.

Choose the participants: Decide on the characteristics of the participants in your study, including their age, gender, health status, and other relevant factors.

Determine the procedures: Decide on the procedures for manipulating the independent variable(s) and measuring the dependent variable(s). Make sure these procedures are valid, reliable, and consistent across participants.

Collect the data: Collect the data using the procedures you have chosen. Record the data accurately and minimize any sources of bias or error.

Analyze the data: Analyze the data using appropriate statistical methods to test your hypothesis.

Draw conclusions: Draw conclusions based on your analysis and determine whether your hypothesis was supported or not. Discuss the implications of your findings and any limitations or future directions for research.

Ending this chapter, we can summarize that, overall, designing an experiment involves careful planning and attention to detail at every stage. If you try to follow these guidelines, you can ensure that your experiment is well-designed and produces valid and reliable results. In the following chapters, we will examine some cases of experimental design. The basic principles remain the same but some details are customized.

28 HOW TO DESIGN AN EXPERIMENT IN PLANT SCIENCE?

Designing an experiment in plant science involves several steps. Here are some general steps to follow:

Identify a research question: Identify a specific research question that you want to answer through your experiment. For example, "Does the amount of fertilizer affect the growth of plants?"

Choose a plant species: Select a plant species that is suitable for your research question and experiment. You should consider factors such as the growth rate, size, and availability of the plant. In general, annual plants have different aspects to consider compared to perennial plants. Similarly, plants propagated by seeds may require a different experimental approach than clonally propagated ones.

Determine experimental variables: Decide on the variables that you will test in your experiment. These variables can include the amount of fertilizer, light exposure, water, temperature, etc. Keep in mind that the more variables you include in your experiment the more complex it gets to implement treatments and analyze the data.

Develop a hypothesis: Based on your research question, develop a hypothesis that predicts the outcome of your experiment. For example, "Increasing the amount of fertilizer will lead to an increase in plant growth." It could even be an open question "How will the plants respond to simultaneous exposure to combined stresses?"

Plan the experiment: Decide on the experimental design, including the number of plants, the type of pot or growing medium, the duration of the experiment, and the method of data collection.

Conduct the experiment: Set up the experiment according to the plan, and monitor the plants throughout the experiment.

Collect and analyze data: Collect data on plant growth and other relevant factors, and analyze the results using statistical methods.

Draw conclusions: Evaluate the results of the experiment and draw conclusions about whether the hypothesis was supported or rejected.

Communicate findings: Communicate your findings through a scientific report or presentation.

It is important to note that the specific steps and details of an experiment in plant science will vary depending on the research question and experimental design. Some basic rules for experimental design apply to all research disciplines, however, there are always minor or more substantial modifications.

29 HOW TO DESIGN AN EXPERIMENT IN ANIMAL SCIENCE?

Designing an experiment in animal science involves several steps. As mentioned earlier, some steps are common with other science disciplines and some other actions are custom for each separate case. Here are some general guidelines to follow:

Define the research question: Identify the specific question you want to answer. This will guide the entire experimental design process.

Choose the animal model: Select an appropriate animal model for your research. Consider factors such as size, lifespan, availability, and cost.

Select a treatment: Determine the treatment or intervention you want to test. This could be a drug, a dietary change, an environmental factor, or something else.

Determine the sample size: Calculate the number of animals needed for your experiment. This will depend on the statistical power you want to achieve and the expected effect size.

Randomization: Randomly assign animals to the treatment and control groups. This helps to eliminate bias and ensure that the groups are comparable.

Control group: Include a control group to compare the effects of the treatment. The control group should be identical to the treatment group except for the intervention.

Blinding: Consider blinding the experimenters and/or the animals to the treatment groups to prevent bias.

Collect data: Collect data on the outcome measures. Use appropriate methods to ensure the validity and reliability of the data.

Statistical analysis: Analyze the data using appropriate statistical tests to determine if there is a significant effect of the treatment.

Conclusion: Draw conclusions based on the results and discuss the implications for animal science.

Last but not least, an important aspect to consider is that it is important to follow ethical guidelines for animal research and obtain appropriate permissions and approvals before conducting any experiments.

30 HOW TO DESIGN AN EXPERIMENT IN ENVIRONMENTAL SCIENCE?

Designing an experiment in environmental science involves a structured approach to test a hypothesis or research question. Here are the general steps to follow:

Formulate a research question: Identify the problem or topic that you want to investigate. This question should be specific and testable.

Conduct a literature review: Gather information from existing studies related to your research question. This will help you understand the current state of knowledge in the field and identify gaps that your study can address.

Develop a hypothesis: Based on your literature review, formulate a clear hypothesis that you will test in your experiment.

Choose a study design: Select an appropriate study design based on your research question and hypothesis. This could be a field study, laboratory experiment, or a combination of both.

Select your study site: Choose a location that is appropriate for your research question and study design. For example, if you are studying the effects of pollution on aquatic life, you might choose a polluted stream and a nearby unpolluted stream for comparison.

Collect data: Collect data using appropriate methods and equipment. Be sure to record all relevant information, including the date, time, location, and any other factors that could affect your results.

Analyze your data: Use statistical methods to analyze your data and test your hypothesis.

Interpret your results: Draw conclusions based on your data analysis and discuss how your results relate to your research question and the existing literature.

Communicate your findings: Share your results with others through publications, presentations, or other means.

It's important to note that the specific steps and methods you use will depend on your research question, study design, and other factors.

31 HOW TO DESIGN AN EXPERIMENT IN SOCIAL SCIENCE?

Designing an experiment in social science requires careful planning and attention to detail. Here are some general steps you can follow:

Develop a research question: Begin by identifying the research question you want to answer. This will help you determine the specific variables that you need to manipulate and measure in your experiment.

Identify the independent and dependent variables: The independent variable is the factor that you manipulate in the experiment, while the dependent variable is the outcome that you measure. Make sure that your variables are well-defined and measurable.

Choose a sample: Decide on the population you want to study and select a representative sample from that population. Make sure your sample size is large enough to produce statistically significant results.

Create a control group: Designate a control group that does not receive the treatment or intervention that you are testing. This will allow you to compare the results of your experimental group to those of the control group.

Randomize: Randomly assign participants to either the experimental or control group to avoid any biases in participant selection.

Develop a procedure: Create a detailed procedure for how you will carry out the experiment, including the steps that participants will follow and how you will measure the dependent variable.

Collect data: Collect data from both the experimental and control groups according to your procedure.

Analyze the data: Use statistical tests to analyze the data you have collected and determine whether the treatment or intervention had a significant effect on the dependent variable.

Draw conclusions: Based on your analysis, draw conclusions about whether your hypothesis was supported and what implications your findings have for the broader field of study.

Write up your results: Summarize your experiment, including your research question, methods, results, and conclusions, in a formal research report. Make sure to follow the standard format and style for your discipline.

32 HOW TO DESIGN AN EXPERIMENT IN HEALTH SCIENCE?

Designing an experiment in health science typically involves the following steps:

Identify the research question: Start by identifying the specific research question you want to answer. This question should be clear, concise, and relevant to the field of health science.

Review existing literature: Conduct a thorough literature review to identify existing knowledge in the area of your research question. This will help you to identify the gaps in knowledge that your study can address.

Develop a hypothesis: Based on your research question and literature review, develop a hypothesis that clearly states your expected outcome.

Choose your study design: There are various study designs to choose from, such as randomized controlled trials, observational studies, cohort studies, case-control studies, and cross-sectional studies. Select the most appropriate design for your research question and hypothesis.

Choose your study population: Identify the target population for your study, taking into account factors such as age, gender, ethnicity, and health status.

Select your sample: Select a representative sample from the target population to ensure that your findings are generalizable to the larger population.

Determine your intervention: If you are conducting an intervention study, determine the intervention that you will use to test your hypothesis.

Collect data: Collect data using appropriate methods such as surveys, interviews, laboratory tests, or medical records.

Analyze data: Analyze the data using appropriate statistical methods to test your hypothesis.

Draw conclusions: Draw conclusions based on your analysis and discuss the implications of your findings for the field of health science.

Communicate your findings: Communicate your findings through academic publications, conferences, or other appropriate channels.

I would like to point out that you should always remember to adhere to ethical considerations and guidelines while conducting your experiment, including obtaining informed consent from participants, maintaining confidentiality, and ensuring participant safety.

33 THE SCIENTIFIC PUBLISHING INDUSTRY

And now, let's discuss the holy grail of scientific research. The scientific publishing industry plays a critical role in the dissemination of scientific knowledge. It serves as a platform for researchers to share their findings and collaborate with their peers. In this section, I will present some thoughts and data so that we explore the publishing industry in science, including its history, current trends, and future directions.

History

The history of scientific publishing dates back to the 17th century when the first scientific journals were established. The Royal Society of London published the first scientific journal, Philosophical Transactions, in 1665. This marked the beginning of a new era in scientific communication, allowing scientists to share their findings with a wider audience. Over time, the number of scientific journals increased, and publishers began to specialize in specific fields.

Current Trends

The scientific publishing industry has undergone significant changes in recent years, driven by advancements in technology and changes in the way research is conducted. The rise of open-access publishing has been one of the most significant trends in the industry. Open-access journals provide unrestricted access to scientific literature, allowing anyone to read and use the research findings. This has led to increased visibility and impact for researchers, especially those in developing countries who previously had limited access to scientific literature.

Another trend is the increasing use of preprint servers. Preprint servers allow researchers to share their work before it has undergone peer review, allowing for faster dissemination of findings. This has been particularly useful during the COVID-19 pandemic, where researchers have been able to rapidly share their findings and collaborate with their peers.

Finally, there has been a growing movement towards transparency and reproducibility in scientific publishing. This includes the use of data and code sharing, pre-registration of studies, and the use of open science practices. These initiatives aim to improve the quality and reliability of scientific research.

Challenges

Despite the many benefits of scientific publishing, there are several challenges that the industry faces. One of the biggest challenges is the high cost of journal subscriptions. Many scientific journals are owned by a small number of publishers, who charge high subscription fees. This has led to the development of alternative publishing models, such as open-access publishing, which aims to make scientific literature more accessible and affordable.

Another challenge is the issue of predatory publishers. These publishers often charge high fees for publishing papers without providing adequate peer review or editorial services. This has led to concerns about the quality and reliability of research published in these journals.

Finally, there are concerns about the lack of diversity and inclusivity in scientific publishing. Women and underrepresented minorities are often underrepresented in scientific publishing, both as authors and as editors. This can lead to a lack of diversity in the perspectives and approaches represented in scientific literature.

Future Directions

The future of scientific publishing is likely to be shaped by continued advancements in technology and changes in the way research is conducted. One possible direction is the continued growth of open-access publishing, which is likely to become increasingly mainstream. Another possible direction is the development of new models for peer review and editorial services, which could lead to faster and more efficient publishing processes.

There is also likely to be a continued focus on transparency and reproducibility in scientific publishing. This may include the use of blockchain technology to ensure the integrity of scientific data and the development of new tools for data sharing and collaboration.

Finally, there is likely to be a continued push for diversity and inclusivity in scientific publishing. This may include efforts to increase the representation of underrepresented groups as authors and editors and to develop new strategies for promoting diversity in scientific literature.

I guess that we all agree that the scientific publishing industry plays a critical role in the dissemination of scientific knowledge. Despite the many challenges it faces, the industry is likely to continue to evolve and adapt to changes in technology and research practices. The future of scientific publishing is likely to be characterized by increased accessibility, transparency, and diversity, leading to a more robust and inclusive scientific publishing world. And we can all contribute towards that direction!

34 HOW TO WRITE A GOOD SCIENTIFIC PAPER?

A fundamental activity of science is the communication of research results to a broad audience starting from the scientific community and expanding to society. Science communication is primarily realized through journal papers. Writing a good scientific paper requires careful planning, thorough research, clear and concise writing, and attention to detail. We have discussed some general tips in a previous chapter and here we will elaborate on good practices for writing a successful scientific paper.

It may seem obvious but the quality of your research is the most important factor in determining whether or not your work will be accepted for publication. Make sure to conduct thorough experiments and analysis, and to use appropriate methodologies. Innovativeness of your work is very important and to achieve that you must have a very goof knowledge of the recent literature.

Your writing should be clear, concise, and easy to understand. Use appropriate scientific terminology, and avoid using overly complex language or jargon.

Choose a journal that is a good fit for your research topic and methodology. Make sure to read the journal's submission guidelines and follow them closely. In the early career stage, I would recommend setting achievable goals and avoiding very high-impact factor journals. Start publishing in more approachable journals and as your level of research and writing advances you can aim higher.

Follow the journal's formatting guidelines for manuscripts, including font, spacing, and citation style. I know it's boring but it gives a very bad impression to the reviewers to ignore journal guidelines. Contrary, a well-prepared manuscript prepares the reviewers for a positive evaluation outcome.

Choose a research question or topic

Identify a research question or topic that is important, interesting, and feasible to investigate. It should be based on a clear understanding of the existing literature and be novel in some way. I suggest discussing your idea with a colleague and a potential end-user to get feedback regarding the actual use of your envisaged work. Scientists are often carried away by fancy science fiction ideas nobody cares about. It's a pity to waste time and resources to produce a useless product, service, or information, isn't it?

Conduct a thorough literature review

Before starting your research, conduct a thorough literature review to identify what has been done in the field and where your study fits in. This will help you to identify research gaps and formulate your research question. I would suggest that you write the introduction right from the beginning. The introduction should provide background information on the topic, a clear statement of the research question or hypothesis, and an overview of the methodology. This would act as a draft version of the manuscript introduction. Later on, after having completed the experiment and data analysis, there will probably be a need to modify the introduction according to some additional approaches you decided to include during your research journey. Focus on reviewing the recent literature and avoid citing publications older than one or two decades. Science evolves rapidly and readers are interested in new information. Be meticulous to report accurately the findings of previous studies because sometimes I read a paper citing my work and I get to wonder "When did I ever say that?". I suggest starting your introduction with the big picture and gradually getting more specific. The last paragraph usually is expected to describe the aims of the study and the main research questions examined.

Develop a clear and concise research design

Clearly define your research design, including your methodology, research subjects, data collection methods, and analysis techniques. This is often the weak point of most experiments! Statistics is not exactly the most popular course at university. When we plan the experiment we sometimes neglect to prepare a robust (or any) experimental design and we remember statistics only after the trial has ended and we want to analyze our results. This way we may get a painful lesson by realizing that we don't fulfill the requirements for statistical analysis (inadequate replications, combined treatments, dissimilarity in the treated objects, etc). And let's keep in mind that a paper without proper statistical analysis of the results is unlikely to get accepted for publication by most scientific journals.

Collect and analyze data

Collect data according to your research design and analyze it using appropriate statistical methods. Be careful to store your data in multiple places the soonest as possible after their collection. Sometimes, we may lose our datasheet by mistake and have a serious flaw in our study. I also suggest writing the date, time, and the person who collected the data so that you can get clarifications when needed.

Write the methods section

The methods section should provide a detailed description of the research design, data collection methods, and analysis techniques. Some journals have specific instructions and requirements that should be respected. Keep in mind that this is not intended to serve as a protocol, so we avoid expressions and details such as "clean your hands before spraying", "use the pipette gently", "add the powder first and then the liquid", etc. For common methods, we may cite a recent paper and mention that we used that protocol in our study and provide just a brief description. The last subsection of "Materials and methods" is commonly the statistical analysis description. Some journals also ask for a subsection regarding reagents and other materials used.

Write the results section

The results section should present your findings clearly and concisely, using tables and figures as needed to illustrate your results. Actually, I first prepare the figures and tables with all the details of the statistical analysis (means, standard errors, letters of statistically significant differences, number or replications, statistical test employed, and level of significance). We should always keep in mind to avoid presenting the same results in both a figure and a table or in multiple visuals. In general, figures are preferable to tables because they are more powerful in communicating the message. Lately, journal paper figures tend to look more and more like PowerPoint presentation slides combining graphs, photos, and explanatory text to be more comprehensive for readers. A figure or table should stand alone, meaning that they have all the necessary information for the reader to understand the results without having to read the whole paper.

After having prepared our visuals, it is really easy to describe in text what we see in figures and tables. It is really helpful for readers to organize the results section into subsections with clear, non-overlapping topics. Results are always presented in the past tense unless otherwise suggested by the journal of interest. First, present the statistically significant differences, then the differences that were over the significance threshold (e.g. 5%, 1%, 0.1%, etc). In the end, mention also the cases in which no differences were observed. Sometimes, we may combine results and discussion in one section but it is generally not advised. Most journal instructions suggest keeping those sections separated to have a clear understanding of what information was produced in our study and what belongs to the literature.

Write the discussion section

The discussion section should interpret your results, place them in the context of the existing literature, and discuss the implications of your findings for the field. You may express the general idea of your findings but please avoid repeating your results. This is a very common mistake that may harm your publication potential. The first paragraph of the discussion could restate the hypothesis of your research and the main findings. Then, use the subsequent paragraphs to discuss one by one all your findings even the statistically non-significant ones. Start with the most important outcomes and continue with the minor observations. Each result should be discussed concerning the recent literature and be accompanied by a suggested interpretation of the underlying mechanisms and the possible implications. A common mistake is to repeat our results and report that they are in agreement or disagreement with previous studies without providing a suggested explanation. The discussion could start with a specific and in-depth examination of the results and end with the broad use of our findings for the stakeholders, society, the environment, the global economy, etc.

Write the conclusion

The conclusion should summarize your main findings, restate the research question or hypothesis, and suggest directions for future research. You could also mention any limitations of the study, what you did to manage them, and how these should be taken into account by readers when considering applying the study outcomes. Keep it simple and provide a take-home message for the end-users of your research results.

Edit and proofread

Once you have completed your paper, edit and proofread it carefully, paying close attention to grammar, spelling, and formatting. You may have been told a million times during school and university studies that those features play a crucial role in the evaluation of our work. It's a pity to present an excellent piece of research and get rejected because of typos! A colleague could help during this step. Share your work with colleagues and ask for feedback. This can help you identify weaknesses in your research and writing, and make improvements before submitting your manuscript for publication. As humans, we are subjective and we magnify our strengths while neglecting our weaknesses. An objective view of our manuscript can only be helpful. Of course, we should ask for help from a colleague with relevant expertise and competence.

Happily, there are also many useful software options for this purpose. If there is an available budget, we may also use the services of expert companies to proofread and format our manuscript before submission to a journal.

If your manuscript is sent out for peer review, carefully consider the reviewer's comments and address them in your revisions. Be respectful and professional in your responses. Commonly, the author declares that all reviewers' suggestions were followed but this is not the case resulting in paper rejection or significant delays in publishing due to repeated rounds of review.

Once your work is published, promote it through social media and other channels to increase its visibility and impact. Prefer ResearchGate and LinkedIn because Facebook may be considered by some people primarily social and to a less extent professional.

These are some very important actions you can take to increase your chances of success in scientific publications. Remember, writing a good scientific paper is a process that takes time and effort. It is important to follow a clear and logical structure and to present your findings clearly and concisely. Later on, I will present some useful resources to help you improve. As in every other aspect of our lives, practice and education make us better.

35 WEBSITES FOR IMPROVEMENT OF SCIENTIFIC WRITING

Scientific writing is an essential aspect of scientific research. It is the means through which scientists communicate their research findings to the scientific community. Scientific writing requires clarity, accuracy, and conciseness. Websites can provide useful resources and tools to help improve scientific writing. In this chapter, we will discuss some of the websites that can be useful for improving scientific writing.

Purdue Online Writing Lab (OWL)
The Purdue Online Writing Lab (OWL) is a popular website that provides comprehensive writing resources. It has a specific section dedicated to scientific writing, which includes tips for organizing scientific papers, formatting scientific papers, and writing abstracts. The OWL also provides resources on grammar, punctuation, and citing sources.

ScienceDocs
ScienceDocs is a website that offers professional scientific editing and proofreading services. They have a team of PhD-level scientists who are experts in scientific writing. ScienceDocs can provide help with scientific manuscripts, grant proposals, conference abstracts, and other scientific documents.

Hemingway Editor
Hemingway Editor is a website that can be used to improve the readability of scientific writing. It can identify long, complex sentences, and highlight adverbs, passive voice, and other writing issues. Hemingway Editor provides a readability score, which can be used to assess the readability of scientific

papers.

American Psychological Association (APA)
The American Psychological Association (APA) is an organization that provides guidelines for scientific writing. The APA website provides resources for formatting scientific papers according to APA style, including guidelines for citing sources, creating references, and formatting headings and subheadings.

Let's always remember that scientific writing is a critical aspect of scientific research. It requires clarity, accuracy, and conciseness. Websites can provide useful resources and tools to help improve scientific writing. The websites discussed in this section, and many others that are available, can be used to improve scientific writing skills, manage references, and format scientific papers. Scientists can use these websites to enhance the quality and impact of their scientific writing.

36 WEBSITES FOR REFERENCE MANAGEMENT IN SCIENTIFIC WRITING

One of the most important aspects of scientific writing is proper referencing. I guess we all agree that this is probably the most boring task when preparing a scientific paper but referencing is a critical component of academic writing as it provides the reader with the necessary information to locate the sources used in the work. However, managing references can be a daunting task, especially for large-scale research projects. In the following pages, I will try to present to you some websites that can help in reference management for scientific writing.

Mendeley
Mendeley is a reference management software that is widely used in the scientific community. It allows users to organize, store, and annotate their research sources. Mendeley can also generate citations and bibliographies in various citation styles, making it easier to format your references in your manuscript.

Zotero
Zotero is a free, open-source reference management software that is similar to Mendeley. It allows users to collect, organize, and cite their research sources. Zotero can also be used as a browser extension, making it easy to save references from the internet.

EndNote
EndNote is a reference management software that is popular among researchers. It allows users to organize, store, and annotate their research sources. EndNote also has a feature that allows users to search for references

online and import them directly into their reference library.

RefWorks

RefWorks is a cloud-based reference management software that allows users to collect, organize, and cite their research sources. RefWorks has a user-friendly interface that makes it easy to use for beginners. It also offers features such as group collaboration and shared folders, making it easier to work with others on research projects.

Papers

Papers is a reference management software that is specifically designed for researchers working on Mac platforms. It allows users to organize, store, and annotate their research sources. Papers can also search for references online and import them directly into the reference library.

Pubmed

Pubmed is a free database that contains over 32 million biomedical literature references. It can be used to search for scientific articles and other references relevant to your research. Pubmed also offers a feature that allows users to save references and generate citations in various citation styles.

Ending this chapter, I would like to point out that proper referencing is critical for scientific writing, and using reference management software can help make the process more efficient and effective. Mendeley, Zotero, EndNote, RefWorks, Papers, and Pubmed are some of the websites that can help in reference management for scientific writing. Using these websites can save time, reduce errors, and make the process of referencing more organized and manageable. Let's hope that in the future all references will be organized automatically and we will focus only on describing our science!

37 SUCCESS IN WRITING RESEARCH GRANTS

Scientists love to research. However, to implement experiments, we need funds for personnel, equipment, and consumables and funds come after heavy-duty grant writing. Writing successful research grants requires careful planning, attention to detail, and effective communication of your research idea and its significance to the funding agency. Here are some tips to help you increase your chances of success.

Choose the right funding agency. Different funding agencies have different priorities and funding criteria. It's important to choose the right agency that is interested in funding research in your area of expertise. For example, in the early career stages of a researcher, when networking is still poor, it is not so realistic to aim at international competitive grants. On the other hand, I would first look for scholarships and grants, planned especially for early-stage researchers.

Read the guidelines carefully. Each funding agency has specific guidelines that must be followed when submitting a grant proposal. Be sure to read the guidelines thoroughly and follow them closely. It's a pity to invest a lot of time and effort in a project proposal that gets rejected for a tiny detail (e.g. a required document not submitted). Contacting the program managing authority for clarifications is always a good idea.

Write clearly and concisely: Write in a clear, concise, and jargon-free language. Avoid using complex sentences and technical terms that may confuse the readers. Use graphs, tables, and images to illustrate your points. Do not take for granted that the reviewers know all the details of background information. Provide all the necessary details to document your proposal.

Develop a clear research question. Your research question should be clearly defined and address a significant gap in knowledge in your field. Make sure you clearly articulate the purpose, objectives, and expected outcomes of your research. Evaluators have limited time for each proposal and we should make it easy for them to get the message and be impressed by our ideas!

Justify the significance of your research. Your grant proposal should explain why your research is important and how it will contribute to the field. Highlight the potential impact of your research on society, the economy, and/or public health. The competition for research grants is huge and sometimes only one out of a hundred proposals gets selected for funding. Having said that, we should design research proposals that indeed are expected to have an impact on society and then present them clearly and with strong evidence to convince the evaluators that they deserve funding.

Outline your research methodology. Clearly outline the methodology you will use to conduct your research. This should include a detailed description of your study design, sample size, data collection methods, and analysis techniques. This will not only help show the evaluators that you know what you are saying but it will also help you be prepared for a realistic and scientifically current experimental plan. If you don't have this during the proposal writing, it may be too late and painful to realize some weaknesses during the project implementation.

Develop a realistic budget. Your budget should be realistic and include all the necessary expenses associated with your research, such as equipment, materials, and personnel. This is a great challenge. The prices for laboratory reagents may rise significantly from the time of grant writing to the time of project implementation, one or two years later. Try to declare some budget fractions for every possible cost category because there are always unforeseen needs that are detected only during project implementation.

Seek feedback. Seek feedback from colleagues, mentors, and funding agency staff before submitting your grant proposal. They may be able to provide valuable insights and suggestions to improve your proposal. Focus on experienced researchers in your company or research center because they would know very well the red tape of the organization and the hot points to be careful with to increase your chances to get the grant.

Proofread and edit. Make sure to proofread and edit your proposal carefully to avoid grammatical errors and typos. To have the time to do that, please do not finish writing your proposal one hour before the submission deadline!

To say once again, submit your proposal on time. In fact, submit your proposal at least two days before the deadline. Keep a copy of your proposal and all supporting documents for your records.

Remember that writing a successful grant proposal takes time and effort. Be prepared to revise and resubmit your proposal if it is not initially successful. This is a very common procedure and the evaluators' rejection letters are very nice lessons for improvement. Do not get angry with them. Instead, study them carefully. Through them, we identify our weaknesses and also realize what they deem important. With persistence and dedication, you can increase your chances of securing funding for your research project. Last but not least, please remember that you may have to submit ten project proposals or more to get one or two grants accepted.

38 EFFICIENT IMPLEMENTATION OF A RESEARCH GRANT

You got the grant, congratulations! Receiving a research grant is an exciting opportunity to explore new ideas, contribute to scientific knowledge, and make a difference in your field. However, a successful grant proposal is just the beginning. Once you receive the grant, you need to effectively implement your research plan to ensure that you achieve your goals, stay within your budget, and meet your deadlines. In this chapter, we will discuss the best practices for implementing a research grant.

Understand the Grant Requirements
Before you begin implementing your research plan, it is important to understand the grant requirements. Read through the grant proposal and any other materials provided by the funding agency carefully. Make sure you understand the scope of the project, the deliverables expected, the timeline, and the budget. If you have any questions or concerns, reach out to the funding agency for clarification. It is important to have a clear understanding of the grant requirements to ensure that you meet them and maintain a good relationship with the funding agency. It is often that a project proposal is written in such a rush that only after selection for funding do we thoroughly read it and realize that some foreseen tasks may be very challenging to implement successfully. We should try to avoid such surprizes at all costs because there is a risk of failure and unpleasant repercussions in our career.

Develop a Detailed Project Plan
Once you understand the grant requirements, develop a detailed project plan. Your plan should include a timeline with specific deadlines for each phase of the project, a budget with estimated costs for each activity, and a list

of the resources you will need. Your plan should be realistic and achievable given the scope of the project and the resources available. It is important to be flexible and willing to adjust your plan as necessary based on new information or unexpected challenges. It is advisable to set reminders in your digital calendar for every deliverable and milestone envisaged in the project proposal.

Establish Communication Channels
Effective communication is critical to the success of a research project. Establish communication channels with your team, the funding agency, and any other stakeholders. Make sure everyone knows how to reach each other, how often they should expect updates, and what information should be included in those updates. Regular communication will help ensure that everyone is on the same page and any issues are addressed quickly. A virtual meeting of the consortium every three months would be an excellent idea. The project coordinator should collect questions from all participating partners as soon as the project starts and communicate them to the Program Managing Authority to get written clarifications. You are encouraged to use written communication for such issues and avoid telephone conversations that may be misunderstood, forgotten, or doubt in the future.

Manage Your Budget
Managing your budget is essential to ensure that you can complete your project within the funding limits. Keep track of all expenses, including salaries, equipment, supplies, and travel. Make sure you have a system in place for requesting and approving expenses, and keep your receipts and invoices organized. If you anticipate going over budget, contact the funding agency as soon as possible to discuss your options. Most research programs nowadays encourage or force the use of an external auditor to ensure that budget management is appropriate.

Collect and Analyze Data
The data you collect is the foundation of your research project. Make sure you have a plan in place for collecting, managing, and analyzing your data. This may include hiring staff, developing data collection tools, and using appropriate software for analysis. Make sure you follow ethical guidelines for data collection and management, and that you have appropriate permissions and consent forms in place. I would recommend using multiple sites to store your data, your PC hard disc, an external hard disc, a cloud storage platform, etc.

Monitor Your Progress
Regularly monitoring your progress is essential to ensure that you stay on

track and meet your deadlines. Establish milestones and check-in points to review your progress and adjust your plan as necessary. Make sure you keep your team and stakeholders informed of your progress and address any issues or concerns that arise promptly. Within each deliverable and task, determine quantifiable progress indicators and try to monthly estimate the overall implementation rate (e.g. 10%, 30%, 80%, etc).

I would like to highlight that implementing a research grant requires careful planning, communication, and management. You are encouraged to keep in mind that by following best practices for project planning, communication, budget management, data collection, and progress monitoring, you can maximize the impact of your research and achieve your goals within the funding limits. Remember to stay flexible, open to feedback, and willing to adjust your plan as necessary to ensure the success of your project.

39 APPLYING FOR A SCIENCE SCHOLARSHIP

During university studies or at the early career stage of a scientist, a scholarship is an excellent step for getting prepared for future research grants but it also has many additional benefits. Science scholarships are a great way for students to pursue their education in science, technology, engineering, and mathematics (STEM) fields. Scholarships can provide financial support to cover tuition, fees, books, and living expenses. Moreover, they can open up opportunities for research, internships, and other educational experiences that can help students build their careers in science. In the following pages, let's see the steps involved in applying for a science scholarship.

Researching Scholarships
The first step in applying for a science scholarship is to research the available opportunities. There are many resources that can help students find science scholarships. Some of these resources include scholarship databases, academic institutions, professional societies, and government agencies. Students should consider their academic background, research interests, and career goals when searching for scholarships.

Meeting Eligibility Criteria
After finding potential scholarships, students should carefully read the eligibility criteria to determine whether they meet the requirements. Eligibility criteria can vary greatly depending on the scholarship and may include factors such as academic performance, financial need, research experience, and citizenship status. If students do not meet the eligibility criteria for a scholarship, they should not waste time applying for it.

Preparing the Application
Once students have identified the scholarships for which they are eligible,

they should begin preparing their application materials. Most science scholarship applications require students to provide transcripts, letters of recommendation, a personal statement, and possibly a research proposal. Students should plan ahead and give themselves enough time to collect all necessary documents, write compelling essays, and refine their research proposals.

Writing a Personal Statement

The personal statement is one of the most important parts of a science scholarship application. This is the student's chance to tell their story and explain why they are passionate about science and deserving of the scholarship. The personal statement should be well-written and concise and should highlight the student's academic achievements, research experience, and career aspirations.

Requesting Letters of Recommendation

Letters of recommendation can provide valuable insight into a student's academic and research potential. Students should select recommenders who are familiar with their academic performance and research experience, and who can speak to their strengths as a candidate for the scholarship. Students should request letters of recommendation well in advance of the application deadline, and provide recommenders with all necessary information and deadlines.

Developing a Research Proposal

Many science scholarships require students to submit a research proposal as part of their application. The research proposal should be well thought out and clearly demonstrate the student's knowledge of the research area. It should include a research question, background information, a hypothesis, a methodology, and expected results. Students should seek feedback from faculty members or research advisors to ensure that their proposal is well-developed and feasible.

Submitting the Application

Once all application materials are ready, students should carefully review the scholarship application instructions and ensure that they have included all required documents. Students should also check that their application is free of grammatical errors and typos. Finally, students should submit their applications before the deadline.

Please keep in mind that applying for a science scholarship can be a challenging and competitive process. However, by researching scholarships, meeting eligibility criteria, preparing application materials, and submitting a well-crafted application, students can increase their chances of receiving financial support for their education and research. With persistence and hard work, students can achieve their goals and build successful careers in science. In the present day, there are numerous opportunities for scholarships as long as we broaden our search in the international market.

40 BECOMING A REVIEWER FOR SCIENTIFIC JOURNALS

During recent decades, we can observe an impressive growth in the number of scientific journals and the number of published papers. For this growth to function properly, there is a huge need for reviewers who will contribute to the selection of manuscripts worth publishing. Becoming a reviewer for scientific journals is an excellent way to contribute to the scientific community while also enhancing your own knowledge and research skills. I will present here the steps to becoming a reviewer for scientific journals, the benefits of reviewing manuscripts, and some tips on how to write a good review.

The first step in becoming a reviewer for scientific journals is to build a strong research profile. You need to have a good understanding of the field and be actively involved in research. You can start by publishing articles in peer-reviewed journals, presenting at conferences, and networking with other researchers. You can also reach out to editors and express your interest in reviewing articles.

Many journals have an online platform where you can register as a reviewer. You can create a profile that highlights your expertise and research interests. You may need to provide a list of your publications, your areas of expertise, and your contact information. Some journals may require you to provide a reference from a senior researcher in the field.

Once you have registered as a reviewer, you may receive invitations to review articles from the journal's editorial team. The invitations may come via email or the journal's online platform. You will typically have a specified time frame to complete the review, usually around 2-4 weeks.

When you accept a review invitation, you will receive the manuscript to review. You should read the manuscript carefully, evaluate the quality of the research, and provide constructive feedback to the authors. Your review should be objective, well-reasoned, and free from personal biases.

There are several benefits to becoming a reviewer for scientific journals. Firstly, it allows you to contribute to the scientific community and support the publication of high-quality research. Secondly, it enables you to stay up-to-date with the latest research in your field, and it can help you to identify new research ideas and collaborations. Finally, it can enhance your own research skills and help you to improve your own writing and presentation skills.

When writing a review, it's important to keep in mind that your feedback should be helpful, constructive, and objective. Here are some tips for writing a good review:

- Start by summarizing the main findings and strengths of the manuscript.
- Be specific in your critique and provide evidence to support your comments.
- Offer suggestions for improvement and provide clear guidance on how to address any weaknesses.
- Keep your tone professional and avoid personal attacks or criticisms.
- Ensure that your review is free from any conflicts of interest.
- Be timely in submitting your review within the given time frame.

In summary, I would like to point out that becoming a reviewer for scientific journals is an excellent way to contribute to the scientific community while also enhancing your own research skills. Consider that by following the steps outlined in this chapter and keeping in mind the tips for writing a good review, you can become a valuable member of the scientific community and support the publication of high-quality research. In the early stage of your career, I suggest that you don't be too picky. Review for conference proceedings or for new journals that have not yet gained high impact factor and prestige. Consider this exercise as a good way to develop skills and prepare for the most famous journals in your field at later stages.

41 JOINING THE EDITORIAL BOARD OF A SCIENTIFIC JOURNAL

There are some well-recognized milestones in the career of a scientist. Joining the editorial board of a scientific journal is a great opportunity for researchers to get involved in the publishing process and contribute to the advancement of their field. Editorial board members are responsible for evaluating the quality of submitted manuscripts, providing feedback to authors, and making decisions about which papers should be published. In this chapter, I will present you the benefits of joining an editorial board, the qualifications and skills required, and the process of applying for and becoming a member of an editorial board.

Benefits of Joining Editorial Boards
Joining an editorial board can be a valuable experience for researchers, offering several benefits. First, it provides an opportunity to stay up-to-date with the latest research in their field. Editorial board members are often sent manuscripts on topics related to their research, which allows them to stay current with emerging research trends and new findings. In fact, Editorial board members are lucky to read new findings before even published!

Second, joining an editorial board allows researchers to build their reputation and gain recognition in their field. Editorial board members are often listed on the journal's website and in the journal itself, which can increase visibility and prestige within the scientific community. This can also lead to invitations to speak at conferences, serve on committees, and participate in other professional activities. Even when a researcher or a university professor is evaluated for a higher position, participation in

Editorial boards is highly weighted.

Third, joining an editorial board can help researchers develop their skills in peer review and manuscript evaluation. As editorial board members, researchers have the opportunity to review and evaluate manuscripts, providing feedback to authors to help them improve their work. This can help researchers develop a better understanding of the publishing process and the criteria used to evaluate scientific research.

Qualifications and Skills

To be considered for an editorial board position, researchers must have a strong publication record in their field and a deep understanding of the research area covered by the journal. They should have a broad knowledge of the latest research trends and emerging findings, as well as experience in peer review and manuscript evaluation. Editorial board members must also possess excellent communication and interpersonal skills, as they will be working closely with authors, reviewers, and the editorial team.

In addition, editorial board members must be able to work effectively in a team environment, be organized and detail-oriented, and be able to manage their time effectively. They must also be committed to the values of the journal and the scientific community, including ethical standards, transparency, and open communication.

Process of Joining an Editorial Board

The process of joining an editorial board varies depending on the journal and the field. Typically, researchers interested in joining an editorial board should start by identifying journals in their field and reviewing the requirements for editorial board membership. This may involve reviewing the journal's website, contacting the editorial team, and attending conferences and meetings where the journal is discussed.

Once researchers have identified a journal they are interested in joining, they should prepare a strong application that highlights their qualifications and experience. This may include a cover letter, a CV, a list of publications, and references from colleagues and peers in their field.

The application will then be reviewed by the editorial team, who will evaluate the applicant's qualifications and fit with the journal's mission and values. If the applicant is selected for an editorial board position, they will be invited to participate in an orientation and training program, which may involve reviewing the journal's policies and procedures, attending editorial meetings, and working closely with the editorial team to learn the ropes of the publishing process.

I would definitely suggest that joining an editorial board can be a rewarding experience for researchers, providing an opportunity to stay up-to-date with the latest research, build their reputation and recognition in their field, and develop their skills in peer review and manuscript evaluation. To be considered for an editorial board position, researchers must have a strong publication record, a deep understanding of their research area, and excellent communication and interpersonal skills. Building experience as a reviewer is definitely helpful. As mentioned in the previous chapter, you are encouraged to get involved in new journals in the early stage of your career, even if they are not among the top respected in your science community to gain experience. It is unlikely that someone is appointed as an editorial member of a top journal without any relevant background. Remember that the stairway to the top begins with the lowest steps.

42 SUCCESS IN PUBLISHING AN E-BOOK

Publishing a book is a milestone for any scientist. Usually, it takes an advanced career and a long experience in science to dare to write a book that is expected to contain the wisdom of the scientist. In modern times, everything goes digital and most books are presented as e-books. There are several steps you can take to maximize your chances of success when publishing an e-book.

Choose a topic that has a high demand but low supply in the market. This means that there is a large audience looking for information on this topic, but there aren't many books available to meet their needs.

Ensure that your e-book is well-written, well-researched, and has a professional cover design. It is recommended to hire an editor and a designer if necessary.

Price your e-book competitively by researching similar titles in your genre and pricing your book accordingly. Avoid pricing too high or too low.

You may use social media platforms and other online marketing channels to promote your e-book. Create a website or blog to build your author brand and promote your book.

Another good idea is to create a mailing list of potential readers by offering a free sample of your e-book in exchange for their email addresses. Use your mailing list to promote your e-book and other related products.

To increase the success of promotional activities for your book you could collaborate with influencers in your niche to reach a wider audience. Ask them to promote your e-book to their followers in exchange for a commission.

It is very useful to use advertising platforms such as Amazon ads, Facebook ads, or Google ads to promote your e-book to a larger audience.

Sometimes it helps to offer bonuses such as a free chapter or a bonus e-book to incentivize readers to purchase your e-book.

In summary, feel confident that by following these steps, you can increase the visibility of your book and reach a wide audience. This way you can expect to have multiple sales of your e-book, ultimately maximizing your profits. And above all, you will enjoy the "feel good and proud" reward!

43 MAKING A SUCCESSFUL PRESENTATION AT A CONFERENCE

The career of a scientist involves frequent participation in conferences and public speeches. Making a successful presentation at a conference can be stressful condition, especially if you are not used to public speaking. However, with the right preparation, you can deliver a great presentation. In this chapter, we will go through the key steps to make a successful presentation at a conference.

The first preparatory action to a successful presentation is to plan it out. You should start by defining the objectives of your presentation. What do you want to achieve? Who is your target audience? What is the key message you want to convey? Once you have a clear idea of your objectives, you can start to structure your presentation.

It is very important to remember that you have a limited amount of time to deliver your presentation. You should, therefore, prioritize the key points and ideas you want to cover. Make sure your presentation flows logically, and each slide builds on the previous one.

The design of your presentation is critical. It's important to create a visually appealing and easy-to-follow presentation. For this purpose, you should use high-quality images and graphs to illustrate your points and use fonts and colors that are easy to read.

The most common mistake in presentations is filling the slides with excessive text. Always keep in mind to avoid overcrowding your slides with too much text or information. Keep it simple and concise, and use bullet points to summarize your ideas. I would recommend presenting up to five lines of text after the title and using two font colors interchangeably. Avoid the combination of red text on a blue background and vice versa because it is very hard to read and in some cases of eye problems impossible to read.

Try it to see what I mean!

I cannot stress more that practicing your presentation is essential. Not only will it help you to memorize your key points, but it will also help you to refine your delivery. Practice in front of a mirror, or record yourself and watch it back to identify areas where you can improve.

The next step of preparation would be practicing your presentation in front of a small audience, such as friends or colleagues. They can provide you with feedback on your delivery and help you to identify any areas that need improvement. In addition, you will have the feeling of presenting to an audience and you will be more relaxed during the official presentation.

And now let's see what happens at the conference. When it comes to delivering your presentation, there are several things you can do to ensure it is successful. Firstly, arrive early and check your equipment to make sure everything is working correctly. This will help to avoid any last-minute technical issues. Many times, there are incompatibility issues due to different software used for the preparation of the presentation and in the conference computer. This may cause minor issues such as text rearrangements in the slides but also can result in more serious problems such as your presentation file not working at all. I usually have the presentation file on a USB stick with me, both in ppt and pdf versions, and also send the files to the organizers by email before arriving at the conference. This way, the chances of failure are minimized.

Before the conference begins, I go up to the stage and I imagine making my presentation to a room full of people. I imagine the feeling of delivering the presentation and looking at the faces of the audience. I walk around the stage and familiarize myself with the surrounding. This is a very useful warm-up!

When the time comes to stand up in front of the audience, take a deep breath and start your presentation with a clear and engaging introduction. This will help to capture the audience's attention and set the tone for the rest of your presentation.

It is crucial that you maintain eye contact with your audience and speak clearly and confidently. Looking at the audience gives you the chance to get instant feedback about your performance and adapt your communication strategy. When you see that people in the room seem bored or frustrated you could ask some questions to the audience to enhance engagement and improve your communication efficiency. For example, "Would you like to ask a question?", "Is everything clear so far?", "Should I speak louder?", "Should I slow down?". Some useful tips are to speak at a steady pace and pause for emphasis when necessary. Stressed scientists tend to talk too fast, and confuse their wording, making it a real challenge for the audience to follow the presentation and get the message.

Finally, end your presentation with a clear summary of your key points and a strong call to action. This will help to reinforce your message and encourage your audience to take action.

We should keep in mind that at every conference there are numerous presentations one after another, with different topics, different visuals, and different speakers and this is exhausting for the audience. Also, some hours of the day are more difficult than others. For example, delivering a presentation in the morning hours you would face a more energetic and interested audience while giving your speech right after lunch you may see several people sleeping in the room, making it hard for you to attract their attention. Therefore, making a successful presentation at a conference requires careful planning, design, and delivery. By following the steps outlined in this chapter, you can deliver a presentation that is engaging, informative, and memorable. Remember to practice, stay calm and confident, and most importantly, have fun!

44 MAKING A SUCCESSFUL INTERVIEW TO SCIENCE MEDIA

One of the most uncomfortable situations for scientists is to give an interview. In my experience, every time the phone rings and a journalist asks for a statement or an interview about a topic of broad interest, most colleagues would search for excuses to avoid getting involved. However, we should keep in mind that media plays a critical role in the communication of scientific discoveries to the public. It is essential to communicate scientific information accurately and effectively to the public. Scientists and researchers are often called upon to provide interviews to various media outlets, including television, radio, newspapers, and magazines. It is, therefore, crucial for scientists to be well-prepared to ensure that they communicate their scientific findings clearly and effectively. This chapter will provide some tips for making a successful interview with science media.

Let's say that you have been contacted by a journalist and agreed to make an interview. Before giving an interview to science media, it is essential to know your audience. Consider the level of knowledge of your audience and tailor your language accordingly. Will you talk to farmers, the general public, or scientists? In any case, avoid using scientific jargon or technical language that may confuse the audience. Instead, use simple language that is easy to understand.

As in every circumstance, preparation is essential for a successful interview. Before the interview, it is advisable to research the media outlet and the journalist who will be conducting the interview. Search for some past interviews of the journalist on youtube or other media and study the way the discussion flows. Is he aggressive? Does he use humor? Does he like to change several subjects? Familiarize yourself with the journalist's style and the type of questions they usually ask. Research your topic thoroughly and prepare key messages that you want to convey during the interview. Anticipate the questions that the journalist may ask and prepare answers in advance.

During the interview, it is important to stay on topic and focus on the key messages that you want to convey. Be concise and to the point, and avoid going off on tangents. It is very common that during the interview, the journalist focuses on a point that you consider of minor importance, and he deviates from the key message you want to communicate. If you are asked a question that is not related to your topic, politely steer the conversation back to your key messages.

Analogies and examples are effective ways to explain complex scientific concepts to a general audience. Use analogies and examples that are familiar to your audience to help them understand your topic. Analogies and examples can also make your interview more interesting and engaging.

Your vibes are crucial in oral communication and confidence and enthusiasm can go a long way in making a successful interview. I suggest that you speak clearly and confidently, and use body language to emphasize your points. It is great to show enthusiasm for your topic and make it clear why it is important. We should try to engage with the journalist and the audience and make our interview a conversation rather than a lecture.

However, we should be cautious because there are several potential pitfalls to avoid during an interview. Be careful to avoid getting drawn into speculation or making claims that are not supported by scientific evidence. Also, keep in mind to avoid making predictions or extrapolating beyond the data. Before the interview think about any political or controversial topics that are not related to your scientific research and that you should avoid in case they arise in the interview.

Even though not among the best times for scientists, giving an interview to science media can be a rewarding experience, allowing them to communicate their research to a wider audience. However, it is essential to prepare in advance and to know your audience. Using analogies and examples, being confident and enthusiastic, and staying on the topic can all contribute to making a successful interview. By avoiding potential pitfalls and focusing on your key messages, you can ensure that your scientific research is accurately and effectively communicated to the public.

45 CREATING A SUCCESSFUL LINKEDIN PAGE

As you probably already know, LinkedIn is a social media platform that focuses on professional networking and career development. With over 700 million users in more than 200 countries, LinkedIn provides a unique opportunity to connect with professionals in our industry, showcase our skills and experience, and potentially land new job opportunities. Let's explore the elements of a successful LinkedIn page and provide tips on how to optimize your profile to stand out to potential employers and professional contacts.

Your profile picture and headline are the first things that people will see when they come across your LinkedIn page. As such, it's important to make a great first impression. When selecting a profile picture, choose a professional headshot that is clear and well-lit. Avoid using selfies or casual photos, as they can give the impression that you are not taking your professional image seriously. Many people use their Facebook photos also on LinkedIn and this is not the best choice.

Your headline should be concise and provide a quick overview of your professional experience and skills. Use keywords that are relevant to your industry, and highlight your areas of expertise.

Your summary section is an opportunity to tell your professional story and highlight your accomplishments. Use this section to showcase your skills, experience, and achievements, and explain why you are passionate about your work. Keep your summary section concise, and use bullet points or short paragraphs to make it easy to read. Use keywords that are relevant to your industry and highlight your unique features to differentiate yourself from other professionals in your field.

The experience section of your LinkedIn profile provides a detailed overview of your work history. When filling out this section, be sure to include your job title, the company you worked for, the dates of your employment, and a brief description of your responsibilities and achievements. Use bullet points to break up long paragraphs and make it easier for readers to scan your profile. Highlight your accomplishments and quantify your results whenever possible.

The education and skills sections of your LinkedIn profile provide an overview of your academic credentials and the skills you have developed throughout your career. When filling out the education section, include the name of the institution you attended, the degree you earned, and the field of study. If you received any honors or awards, be sure to highlight them. The skills section should include a list of your top skills, with the most important ones listed first. Be sure to include both hard (e.g. computer programming) and soft (group work) skills, and use keywords that are relevant to your industry.

Recommendations and endorsements are an important part of building a successful LinkedIn profile. These endorsements provide social proof that you are a talented professional who is respected by your peers and colleagues.

When requesting recommendations, choose people whom you have worked closely with and who can speak to your skills and experience. When endorsing others, only endorse people for skills that you have seen them demonstrate.

The power of LinkedIn lies in its ability to connect you with other professionals in your industry. You may use the platform to connect with people you have worked with in the past, as well as people you admire and want to learn from. It is a great opportunity to engage with your network by sharing articles, commenting on other people's posts, and participating in industry groups. This will help you stay top of mind and build relationships with other professionals in your field.

LinkedIn is my favorite professional networking medium and I invest a lot of time to grow my network and discuss collaboration ideas. I also often post job opportunities to help match the employers to candidates. I would say that a successful LinkedIn page showcases your skills, experience, and achievements, and makes it easy for potential employers and professional contacts to learn more about you. Try to use some of the tips outlined in this chapter to optimize your profile and stand out from other professionals in your industry, but above all to network with other scientists around the world!

46 MAKING A SUCCESSFUL SCIENCE VIDEO ON YOUTUBE

In recent years, the popularity of YouTube has exploded, with millions of people visiting the site each day to watch videos on a variety of topics. One area that has seen significant growth is science education, with many creators producing content that engages and educates viewers about scientific concepts. Making a successful science video on YouTube requires a combination of knowledge, skill, and creativity. In the following pages, we will explore the key steps to making a successful science video on YouTube.

The first step to making a successful science video is to plan your content. You should begin by choosing a topic that is both interesting and informative. It is important to consider your audience and tailor your content to their level of knowledge and interest in the topic. Also, you need to research your topic thoroughly and make sure you have a clear understanding of the subject matter. Next, consider the format of your video. Will it be a lecture-style presentation, a demonstration, or a combination of both? Consider using visual aids, such as diagrams or animations, to help illustrate complex concepts.

Once you have planned your video, it's time to start scripting. A well-written script is crucial to the success of your video. It will help you stay on track and ensure that you cover all the necessary information. When writing your script, use clear and concise language. Avoid technical jargon and explain any scientific terms or concepts in simple, easy-to-understand language. Keep your script engaging and use humor, anecdotes, or interesting examples to capture your audience's attention.

Now let's discuss the core of this activity which is, what else, filming your video. To ensure a high-quality video, use a good-quality camera and microphone. Many videos on YouTube have been recorded on mobile phones but if you can afford to buy shooting equipment it would be even better. Consider your lighting and background, and ensure that your video is well-framed and in focus. Actually, for this purpose, we usually use professionals to ensure a high-quality result. In the end, we cannot be experts in everything!

When filming, try to be as natural and relaxed as possible. Speak clearly and at a comfortable pace. Don't be afraid to use hand gestures or other nonverbal cues to emphasize your points.

After filming, it's time to edit your video. Use editing software to trim and arrange your footage, add music or sound effects, and insert any visual aids or animations. Again, consider collaborating with professionals. When editing, keep in mind the length of your video. YouTube viewers tend to have short attention spans, so aim for a video length of between 5-10 minutes. Make sure your video is well-paced, and avoid any long or boring sections.

The final step to making a successful science video is to upload and promote your video. It is recommended to use relevant keywords and tags to help your video appear in search results. It would help if you share your video on social media platforms and with relevant communities or groups.

What I often observe that famous YouTubers do, is encourage viewers to leave comments and feedback, and they try to respond to any questions or comments promptly. This will help build engagement and increase your audience. Making a successful science video on YouTube requires careful planning, scripting, filming, and editing. Here I presented some ideas that may be helpful for you to create engaging and informative videos that educate and entertain your audience. Keep in mind that with time and practice, you can build a following and become a respected science educator on YouTube.

47 MAKING A SUCCESSFUL SCIENCE POST ON FACEBOOK

Facebook is traditionally used for social communication. This is a nice way to share photos of our family vacation, catch up with old friends and wish them a happy birthday! In recent years, social media platforms such as Facebook have also become important tools for scientists to disseminate their research findings, share their perspectives, and engage with a wider audience. Mixing social with professional communication in the same medium might be considered a controversial issue but, in the end, this is a decision that each of us will take independently. In any case, making a successful science post on Facebook requires more than just sharing a link or a paper title. In this chapter, we will discuss some of the key strategies that can help you make your science post successful.

The first step in making a successful science post on Facebook is to know your audience. This means understanding the demographics, interests, and preferences of the people you are targeting. Are they scientists, students, or the general public? What kind of content do they prefer? What are their interests and motivations? Once you have a clear understanding of your audience, you can tailor your posts accordingly. For example, if your audience is primarily students, you might want to use more accessible language and focus on the practical applications of your research.

Visuals such as images, videos, and infographics are more engaging than text alone. When making a science post on Facebook, try to include relevant visuals that can help convey your message more effectively. For example, if you are sharing a research paper, you might include a graph or a chart that illustrates your findings.

As in every incident of science communication, when making a science post on Facebook, it is important to keep your message simple and concise.

Avoid using jargon or technical terms that might be difficult for your audience to understand. Instead, use plain language and focus on the key takeaways from your research. Remember that engaging with your audience is key to making a successful science post on Facebook. We should try to respond to comments and questions, and encourage our followers to share their thoughts and opinions. This can help create a sense of community and foster dialogue around our research.

The timing of your science post on Facebook can also affect its success. Try to post during peak hours when your audience is most likely to be online. You can use Facebook Insights to determine when your followers are most active. Hashtags are a great way to make your science post more discoverable on Facebook. Use relevant hashtags that are popular among your audience to increase the visibility of your post.

It's not rocket science, however, making a successful science post on Facebook requires a combination of strategies such as knowing our audience, using visuals, keeping it simple, engaging our audience, timing our post, and using hashtags. These are some ideas to consider so that we can effectively communicate our research findings and engage with a wider audience on Facebook.

48 MAKING A SUCCESSFUL SCIENCE POST ON TWITTER

Twitter has become a vital platform for scientists to share their research findings and engage with other scientists and the general public. However, making a successful science post on Twitter requires a specific set of skills and strategies. Let's discuss in this chapter the steps scientists can take to make successful science posts on Twitter.

Before posting anything, scientists should define their objectives. Is it to promote their research? To share their expertise? To engage with other scientists? To communicate scientific concepts to the general public? Once the objective is clear, it becomes easier to craft a message that aligns with that objective. We should keep in mind that Twitter has a strict character limit of 280 characters. Therefore, scientists should craft a message that is concise, clear, and compelling. For example, the message should include a catchy headline, a link to the research article, and relevant hashtags. It should also be written in plain language that is accessible to both scientists and non-scientists.

As also mentioned in previous communication chapters, visuals such as images, infographics, and videos can enhance the impact of a science post on Twitter. They can also help to break up text-heavy messages and make them more visually appealing. Scientists should use visuals that are relevant to their message and of high quality. Another key point to remember is that the timing of a science post on Twitter can have a significant impact on its success. Scientists should post their messages when their target audience is most active on the platform. This could be during weekdays, during business hours, or specific events such as conferences or webinars. They should also consider the time zone of their audience.

Engaging with followers is crucial for building a strong presence on

Twitter. We should try to respond to comments, retweet relevant messages, and follow other scientists in their field. We can also participate in Twitter chats or create our own to engage with our audience. To determine the impact of a science post on Twitter, scientists should track metrics such as the number of likes, retweets, comments, and clicks on the link. You can use social media analytics tools to measure these metrics and adjust your strategies accordingly.

Twitter has become a vital platform for scientists to share their research findings and engage with other scientists and the general public. Some important points to keep in mind for successful communication are defining the objective, crafting a compelling message, using visuals, choosing the right time to post, engaging with followers, and measuring the impact.

49 CREATING A SUCCESSFUL SCIENCE POST ON INSTAGRAM

Among other social media platforms, Instagram has also revolutionized the way we communicate. Science communication has become more accessible and engaging than ever before. Instagram, with its visual appeal and expansive reach, has become a powerful tool for science communicators to connect with their audience. Here I will present the key elements for creating a successful science post on Instagram. Some points are common with the other social media we discussed in previous chapters but are mentioned also here so that you have a complete and concentrated view of each tool when you decide to use it.

Before you start creating content, it's essential to identify your target audience. Who are they, and what kind of content do they enjoy? Understanding your audience will help you tailor your content to their interests and preferences. For instance, if your target audience is primarily young adults, you might use pop culture references or trending hashtags to grab their attention.

Science can be complex, but our posts don't have to be. We should better keep our language simple and easy to understand. We can also use visual aids such as graphs, charts, or diagrams to help explain complex concepts. Remember, your goal is to make science accessible to everyone, not just scientists. Instagram is a visual platform, so our posts should be visually appealing. For that purpose, we can use high-quality images or videos to grab our audience's attention. It is also advisable that we experiment with different layouts, fonts, and colors to create a unique aesthetic that represents our brand.

Science can often seem distant or disconnected from our everyday lives. It will be really helpful if we make our content relatable by highlighting the real-world applications of scientific research. We could show how science impacts our daily lives and the world around us. Social media is a two-way conversation. Let's encourage our audience to engage with our content by asking questions, using polls or quizzes, or responding to comments. Of course, it is important to respond promptly to our followers' comments and feedback and create a community around our content.

I would like to stress that consistency is key to building a loyal following. It is advisable to post regularly and at a frequency that works for you and your audience. You may use analytics to track engagement and adjust your content strategy as needed. In addition, hashtags are a powerful tool for reaching new audiences. I suggest that you use relevant hashtags to increase the visibility of your posts and connect with like-minded individuals. You could even consider researching popular science hashtags or creating your unique hashtag to create a sense of community around your content.

Some important elements to keep in mind for creating a successful science post on Instagram are creativity, simplicity, and engagement. Remember to stay true to your brand, experiment with different approaches, and have fun while sharing the wonders of science with the world.

50 INTRODUCTION TO SCIENCE COMMUNICATION ON TIKTOK

I know what you are thinking. Oh my god! Another social media platform I have to deal with! With so much communication I will forget my science! I sympathize with you. Please, show some more patience and we will change the subject in the next chapter. For now, let's not ignore that TikTok is a relatively new social media platform that has become increasingly popular among young people in recent years. While the app is often associated with funny videos, it is also a great platform for science communication because of its popularity and directness. In this chapter, we will explore the key components of creating a successful science post on TikTok.

The first step to creating a successful science post is to identify your niche. This could be a specific scientific topic that you are passionate about or an area of research that you are currently working on. Once you have identified your niche, you can begin to research popular trends and hashtags related to your area of interest. One of the key components of a successful science post on TikTok is creating engaging content. This means that your content should be visually appealing and easy to understand. You can use a variety of techniques to make your content more engaging, such as using animations, music, and special effects.

When it comes to science communication on TikTok, it's important to keep your content simple and easy to understand. Avoid using technical jargon or complex scientific concepts that may be difficult for your audience to understand. Instead, focus on breaking down complex topics into simple, easy-to-understand terms. Incorporating humor into your science posts can be an effective way to engage your audience and make your content more relatable. This can be done by using memes or humorous anecdotes related to your topic. However, it's important to use humor in a way that is appropriate and respectful.

Please, keep in mind that building a following on TikTok takes time and effort. To build a following, it's important to consistently create and share engaging content. We can also use popular hashtags related to our niche to help our content reach a wider audience. Interacting with our followers by responding to comments and messages can also help to build a sense of community around our content. Measuring the success of our science posts on TikTok can be done in several ways. One way to measure success is by tracking the number of views and likes our posts receive. We can also track engagement by monitoring comments and shares. Additionally, we can use analytics tools provided by TikTok to track audience demographics and engagement.

In summary, some important points for efficient science communication on TikTok are identifying our niche, crafting engaging content, keeping it simple, incorporating humor, building a following, and measuring success.

51 UNDERSTANDING INTELLECTUAL PROPERTY RIGHTS

Intellectual Property Rights (IPRs) are the legal rights that protect creations of the human mind. These creations include inventions, literary and artistic works, symbols, names, and images used in commerce. IPRs provide the creators of these works with exclusive rights to use, sell, or license their creations for a specific period. The purpose of preparing this chapter was to provide an overview of different types of intellectual property rights, their importance, and the challenges associated with their protection.

Types of Intellectual Property Rights
The four main types of IPRs are patents, trademarks, copyrights, and trade secrets. Each type of IPR offers different protection to the creators and is governed by different laws.

Patents protect inventions, such as machines, processes, and products. They provide the inventor with exclusive rights to prevent others from making, using, or selling the invention for a certain period, usually 20 years from the date of filing the patent application.

Trademarks protect symbols, names, and designs used to identify and distinguish goods and services in the market. Trademark owners have exclusive rights to use their mark and can take legal action against others who use it without permission.

Copyrights protect original works of authorship, such as literary, artistic, and musical works. Copyright owners have exclusive rights to reproduce, distribute, and display their works for a certain period, usually the life of the author plus 70 years.

Trade secrets protect confidential information, such as formulas, processes, and customer lists, which give businesses a competitive advantage.

The owners of trade secrets have exclusive rights to prevent others from using or disclosing the information without permission.

Importance of Intellectual Property Rights
IPRs play a crucial role in promoting innovation, creativity, and economic growth. They encourage creators to invest time, money, and resources in developing new ideas and technologies by providing them with legal protection and financial incentives. IPRs also help businesses to differentiate their products and services from those of their competitors, which creates a level of trust and reliability in the market.

Challenges in Protecting Intellectual Property Rights
The protection of IPRs faces several challenges, including counterfeiting, piracy, and infringement. Counterfeiting is the production and sale of fake or imitation goods that infringe on trademarks and copyrights. Piracy is the unauthorized distribution of copyrighted works, such as movies, music, and software. Infringement is the unauthorized use of patented inventions or trade secrets.

These challenges are becoming increasingly difficult to overcome due to the rapid pace of technological advancements and globalization. The internet has made it easier for counterfeiters and pirates to reach a wider audience, and the lack of effective international laws and enforcement mechanisms has made it harder to protect IPRs in different countries.

In summary, I would say that intellectual property rights are essential for promoting innovation, creativity, and economic growth. They provide creators with legal protection and financial incentives to invest in developing new ideas and technologies. However, the protection of IPRs faces several challenges, including counterfeiting, piracy, and infringement, which require effective international laws and enforcement mechanisms to overcome.

52 SUCCESS IN PATENTS: STRATEGIES FOR INNOVATION AND PROTECTION

Most of us are not very familiar with this issue, but patents are legal instruments that provide inventors with exclusive rights to use, sell, and license their inventions for a specified period. Patents have become a key driver of innovation and economic growth, providing inventors with the necessary incentives to invest in research and development. In the following pages, we will discuss strategies for achieving success in patents, including the importance of innovation, patentability criteria, patent filing and prosecution, and patent portfolio management.

The Importance of Innovation

Innovation is the foundation of successful patents. Patents are granted for novel and non-obvious inventions that have utility in the marketplace. Therefore, inventors must focus on developing products, processes, and services that are truly innovative and provide a competitive advantage. Innovation requires a deep understanding of market needs and trends, as well as a willingness to take risks and experiment with new ideas. Additionally, inventors should conduct thorough prior art searches to ensure that their inventions are novel and non-obvious.

Patentability Criteria

In order to obtain a patent, an invention must meet several criteria, including novelty, non-obviousness, and utility. Novelty requires that the invention is new and has not been publicly disclosed before the filing date of the patent application. Non-obviousness requires that the invention is not obvious to a person having ordinary skill in the relevant field of technology. Utility requires that the invention has a useful purpose and is not frivolous.

Patent Filing and Prosecution

The process of obtaining a patent can be lengthy and complex, involving several steps such as patent searching, drafting, filing, and prosecution. Patent searching involves conducting a comprehensive search of prior art to determine the novelty and non-obviousness of the invention. Patent drafting involves preparing a detailed description of the invention and its claims. Patent filing involves submitting the patent application to the relevant patent office. Patent prosecution involves responding to the patent office's requests for additional information or amendments to the application.

Successful patent prosecution requires a thorough understanding of the patent system and the ability to communicate effectively with the patent examiner. Inventors should be prepared to make amendments to the application and argue for the novelty and non-obviousness of the invention. Additionally, inventors should be aware of the deadlines and timelines involved in the patent application process to ensure that they do not miss any important deadlines.

Patent Portfolio Management

Successful patent portfolio management involves developing and maintaining a portfolio of patents that provides a competitive advantage in the marketplace. Inventors should focus on developing patents that protect their core technology and provide a barrier to entry for competitors. Additionally, inventors should regularly review and assess their patent portfolio to identify areas for improvement and identify potential licensing and enforcement opportunities.

Let's remember that achieving success in patents requires a deep understanding of the patent system and a commitment to innovation. Inventors must focus on developing truly innovative products, processes, and services that meet the patentability criteria. Additionally, inventors must be prepared to navigate the complex patent application process and manage their patent portfolio effectively. If you follow these strategies as inventors, you can protect your intellectual property, providing a competitive advantage and driving innovation and economic growth.

53 WEBSITES TO PATENT YOUR FINDING: A GUIDE TO PROTECTING YOUR INTELLECTUAL PROPERTY ONLINE

In the digital age, intellectual property protection has become an increasingly important issue for individuals and businesses alike. With the proliferation of websites and other online platforms, it is now easier than ever to share and distribute creative works, but it has also become easier for others to copy or infringe on those works. For innovators and inventors, this means that securing a patent is a crucial step in protecting their intellectual property. Fortunately, there are several websites that can help with the patenting process, and in this chapter, we will discuss some of the most popular and effective options.

United States Patent and Trademark Office (USPTO)
The USPTO is the main government agency responsible for granting patents in the United States. Its website offers a wealth of information and resources for inventors, including a database of existing patents, instructions on how to file a patent application, and guidance on how to conduct a patent search. The USPTO website also provides a portal for submitting patent applications and paying fees online, which can save inventors time and effort.

Google Patents
Google Patents is a search engine specifically designed to help users find patents and patent applications from around the world. The website's search capabilities are powerful and flexible, allowing users to search by keyword, inventor name, patent number, and more. Google Patents also provides

access to PDF copies of patents, making it easy to review and analyze existing patents as part of the research process.

PatentLens

PatentLens is a free, open-access patent search platform created by the non-profit organization, Cambia. The website offers a range of tools and resources for patent search and analysis, including a database of over 15 million patents from around the world. PatentLens also provides a visual search tool that allows users to explore patent data using interactive maps and graphs.

PatSnap

PatSnap is a paid patent search and analytics platform that provides a range of tools for patent search, analysis, and management. The website's search capabilities are powerful and flexible, allowing users to search by keyword, inventor name, patent number, and more. PatSnap also provides a range of analytics tools that can help inventors understand the patent landscape and make informed decisions about their own patent applications.

FreePatentsOnline

FreePatentsOnline is a free patent search engine that allows users to search over 10 million patents from around the world. The website's search capabilities are easy to use, with options to search by keyword, inventor name, patent number, and more. FreePatentsOnline also provides a range of tools and resources for patent search and analysis, including the ability to save and organize search results.

In summary, we realize that there are several websites available for inventors looking to patent their findings. These websites offer a range of tools and resources for patent search, analysis, and management, making it easier than ever to protect intellectual property online. Whether using a free search engine like Google Patents or a paid platform like PatSnap, inventors should take advantage of these resources to ensure that their innovations are protected and secure.

54 THE IMPORTANCE OF SCIENTIFIC DATABASES

Scientific databases are an essential component of modern scientific research. They serve as repositories of information that can be used to generate new knowledge and insights. This chapter will provide an overview of scientific databases, their importance, and how they are used in scientific research.

What are scientific databases?
Scientific databases are collections of scientific data, often organized in a structured way that makes it easy to search and retrieve information. They can contain a wide range of data, including experimental results, observational data, and theoretical models.

Scientific databases may be designed to serve a particular research community or to cover a broad range of scientific disciplines. They can be managed by government agencies, academic institutions, or private companies. Many scientific databases are publicly accessible, while others are restricted to authorized users.

Why are scientific databases important?
Scientific databases are essential for scientific research in several ways. First, they provide a way to store and manage large amounts of data. This can be particularly important for research projects that generate a large amount of data, such as those involving high-throughput sequencing or large-scale simulations.

Second, scientific databases provide a way to share data with other researchers. By making data available to others, scientists can promote collaboration and facilitate the validation of results.

Third, scientific databases can help scientists discover new insights and patterns in data. By providing a way to search and analyze large datasets, scientific databases can help scientists identify correlations and trends that might not be apparent otherwise.

How are scientific databases used in scientific research?
Scientific databases are used in a wide range of scientific research fields, including biology, physics, chemistry, and environmental science. Some examples of how scientific databases are used include:

Genomics: Genomic databases such as GenBank and the European Nucleotide Archive provide a way to store and share DNA and RNA sequence data. These databases are used by researchers to identify new genes and to compare sequences across different species.

Proteomics: Proteomic databases such as the Protein Data Bank and UniProt provide a way to store and share information about proteins. These databases are used by researchers to identify protein structures and to study protein interactions.

Climate science: Climate databases such as the National Oceanic and Atmospheric Administration's (NOAA) National Centers for Environmental Information (NCEI) provide a way to store and share climate data. These databases are used by researchers to study climate patterns and to model future climate scenarios.

Neuroscience: Neuroscience databases such as the Allen Brain Atlas provide a way to store and share information about the brain. These databases are used by researchers to study the structure and function of the brain.

Challenges in scientific database management
Managing scientific databases can be challenging for several reasons. First, scientific data can be complex and heterogeneous, making it difficult to develop a standardized way to store and retrieve data.

Second, scientific data can be very large, making it challenging to store and process the data efficiently. This can be particularly true for datasets generated by high-throughput sequencing or large-scale simulations.

Third, scientific databases may need to comply with various regulations and policies, such as data privacy laws or intellectual property regulations.

Scientific databases are essential for modern scientific research. They provide a way to store and manage large amounts of data, share data with other researchers, and discover new insights and patterns in data. While managing scientific databases can be challenging, the benefits of using them far outweigh the costs.

55 USEFUL SOFTWARE FOR SCIENTISTS

The field of science has greatly benefited from advancements in technology, particularly software tools that enable researchers to conduct experiments, analyze data, and share their findings with the scientific community. In this chapter, we will discuss some of the most useful software tools for scientists, from data analysis software to scientific writing tools.

Scientific Data Management Systems
Scientific Data Management Systems (SDMS) are increasingly becoming essential for scientific research as data volumes grow and become more complex. One example of an SDMS is LabKey Server, which provides researchers with tools for data integration, management, and analysis. LabKey Server also includes features such as secure access controls, audit trails, and data versioning. Another example is the Integrated Rule-Oriented Data System (iRODS), which allows researchers to store, manage, and share data across multiple sites and organizations. iRODS includes automated data workflows, advanced search and discovery features, and a suite of APIs for integrating with other research tools. Finally, the Globus research data management platform provides researchers with a secure and reliable way to move, share, and discover data across different institutions and computing systems. It also offers features such as automated data transfer and synchronization, cloud integration, and data publication services. In summary, SDMS provide researchers with powerful tools for managing their data throughout the research lifecycle, from collection and analysis to publication and sharing.

Data Analysis Software
Data analysis software is an essential tool for scientists, as it allows them to make sense of large data sets and extract meaningful insights from them.

Here are some of the most popular data analysis software tools:

- MATLAB: MATLAB is a numerical computing software that is widely used in scientific research. It offers a variety of tools for data analysis, including statistical analysis, data visualization, and machine learning.

- R: R is a programming language that is used for statistical computing and graphics. It is open-source software, which means it is freely available and can be customized to suit the needs of individual researchers.

- Python: Python is a popular programming language for scientific computing and data analysis. It offers a wide range of libraries and tools for data manipulation, visualization, and analysis.

- SPSS: SPSS (Statistical Package for the Social Sciences) is a statistical analysis software that is widely used in social science research. It offers a variety of tools for data analysis, including descriptive statistics, correlation analysis, and regression analysis.

Scientific Writing Tools

Scientific writing is a critical aspect of scientific research, and it requires precision, clarity, and accuracy. Here are some of the most useful scientific writing tools:

- LaTeX: LaTeX is a document preparation system that is widely used in scientific research. It allows researchers to create high-quality documents with mathematical symbols, equations, and graphs.

- Overleaf: Overleaf is an online LaTeX editor that allows researchers to collaborate on scientific documents in real-time. It offers a variety of templates and tools for scientific writing.

- Mendeley: Mendeley is a reference management software that allows researchers to organize and manage their research papers, articles, and other documents. It also offers a variety of tools for citing sources and creating bibliographies.

- Grammarly: Grammarly is a writing assistant that checks for grammar, spelling, and punctuation errors. It is an essential tool for scientific writing, as it helps to ensure that documents are error-free and easy to read.

Visualization Software
Visualization software is another essential tool for scientists, as it allows them to communicate their findings effectively. Here are some of the most popular visualization software tools:

- Graphpad Prism: Prism offers a great combination of data statistical analysis with the most popular methods that are suitable for quantitative and categorical data and an excellent platform for preparing graphs that are ideal for scientific papers.

- Tableau: Tableau is a data visualization software that allows researchers to create interactive dashboards and visualizations. It is widely used in scientific research, as it allows researchers to explore and analyze data in real-time.

- D3.js: D3.js is a JavaScript library that is used for creating interactive data visualizations on the web. It offers a wide range of tools for data manipulation, visualization, and animation.

- ggplot2: ggplot2 is a data visualization package for R that allows researchers to create high-quality graphics and visualizations. It offers a variety of tools for data visualization, including scatter plots, line charts, and bar charts.

In summary, I would like to highlight that there are many useful software tools available to scientists, ranging from data analysis software to scientific writing tools and visualization software. If they familiarize themselves with and use these tools, researchers can conduct experiments, analyze data, and communicate their findings effectively with the scientific community. As technology continues to advance, we can expect to see even more powerful and useful software tools emerge that will further enhance the field of scientific research.

56 THE IMPORTANCE OF THE ENGLISH LANGUAGE FOR SCIENTISTS

Imagine how complicated international communication must have been some centuries ago when learning to speak foreign languages was meaningful only for a very small fraction of the population to serve commercial activities. During recent decades, we are happy to see people developing a new mentality of feeling like citizens of the world, embracing multiculturism, and being open to interacting with men and women of different races, from other continents, and civilizations for social or professional purposes. As the language of international communication, English has become a critical tool for scientists. It enables researchers from all over the world to communicate effectively, exchange ideas, and collaborate on research projects. Let's discuss here some aspects regarding the importance of English for scientists and how it can contribute to scientific progress.

In the field of science, communication is essential. Scientists need to communicate their findings, discuss their research, and collaborate with others. English has become the most common language of the scientific community, allowing scientists from different countries to communicate effectively. The ability to communicate in English also opens up opportunities for scientists to attend international conferences, present their research, and publish their work in high-impact journals.

Collaboration is an essential aspect of modern scientific research. Collaboration allows scientists to share their expertise, resources, and ideas. Collaboration can lead to breakthroughs in research and scientific discoveries. English plays a critical role in facilitating scientific collaboration. It enables scientists from different countries to work together on research projects, share data, and discuss their findings.

Scientific research is a global endeavor, and English is the language of scientific literature. Most scientific journals, books, and research papers are written in English. Access to these resources is essential for scientists to keep up-to-date with the latest research findings, techniques, and trends in their field. Knowledge of English allows scientists to access these resources, read and understand scientific publications, and contribute to the scientific community.

In the competitive world of science, career advancement depends on publication and recognition. The ability to write and communicate in English is essential for scientists to publish their work in high-impact journals, present their research at international conferences, and network with other scientists. English proficiency is often a requirement for scientific positions, especially in international organizations and institutions. When I was considering applying for a vacancy in the International Olive Council, the top organization in the world in my field of research, I realized that it was desired to have good communication skills in English, French, and Arabic to efficiently communicate with the member states as well as Spanish, since the headquarters are in Madrid.

In summary, I would like to say that the importance of English for scientists cannot be overstated. It is essential for communication, collaboration, access to resources, and career advancement. As the language of international communication, English enables scientists to participate in the global scientific community and contribute to scientific progress. We as scientists should invest in improving our English language skills to enhance our scientific careers and make significant contributions to the scientific community.

57 SOFTWARE FOR ENGLISH EDITING: TOOLS AND TECHNIQUES

In today's digital age, English language editing has become a vital component of written communication. Whether it is academic research papers, business reports, or personal communication, good writing skills are essential to convey ideas effectively. And let's be honest, most of us are not exactly fluent in English writing or speaking. However, the good news is that with the advent of technology, a wide range of software tools and techniques are available to help writers improve their written communication skills. In the following pages, we will discuss various software tools and techniques that can be used for English language editing. I definitely benefit from their use in my work.

Grammar Checkers
One of the most widely used software tools for English language editing is the grammar checker. Grammar checkers can help identify grammatical errors, spelling mistakes, punctuation errors, and other common errors in written communication. Some popular grammar checkers include Grammarly, ProWritingAid, and Ginger.

Style Checkers
In addition to grammar checkers, style checkers can help writers improve their writing style. Style checkers can identify common issues such as repetitive phrases, passive voice, and wordiness. Some popular style checkers include Hemingway Editor and StyleWriter.

Plagiarism Checkers

Plagiarism is a serious concern in academic research and other forms of written communication. Plagiarism checkers can help writers identify potential instances of plagiarism by comparing the text to a vast database of existing content. Some popular plagiarism checkers include Turnitin and PlagScan.

Language Translation Software
English is a global language, and many writers need to communicate with people who speak different languages. Language translation software can help writers translate their written communication into different languages quickly. Some popular language translation software tools include Google Translate and SDL Trados.

Text-to-Speech Software
Sometimes, hearing the text can help writers identify errors that they might miss while reading. Text-to-speech software can read the text aloud, allowing writers to hear their writing and identify issues such as awkward phrasing or incorrect grammar. Some popular text-to-speech software tools include NaturalReader and ReadSpeaker.

Closing this chapter I would like to summarize that English language editing software tools and techniques can be useful for writers who want to improve their written communication skills. Grammar checkers, style checkers, plagiarism checkers, language translation software, and text-to-speech software are some popular tools that writers can use to enhance their writing skills. These software tools are not a replacement for human editors, but they can help identify common errors and improve writing style. I believe that it is safe to predict that as technology continues to evolve, we can expect more advanced software tools to become available, making English language editing even more accessible and effective.

58 ETHICS IN SCIENCE

In life, there are so many rules we have to follow, some are formal laws and some others are moral instructions based on tradition or what is perceived as good practice. An inconvenient topic in science is related to ethical behavior. Ethics in science is a complex and multifaceted topic that encompasses a range of ethical considerations that arise throughout the scientific process. From research design and data collection to publication and dissemination, scientists must grapple with a range of ethical issues that can have profound implications for individuals, communities, and society as a whole. Let's discuss here some of the key ethical issues that arise in science and offer guidance for how scientists can navigate these issues ethically and responsibly.

Responsible Conduct of Research
One of the foundational principles of ethics in science is the responsible conduct of research. This involves a commitment to conducting research in a manner that is both rigorous and ethical, with an emphasis on transparency, honesty, and integrity. Scientists have a responsibility to design scientifically valid studies, minimize risks to research subjects, and ensure that the data collected is accurate and reliable. This requires careful attention to study design, data collection methods, and the selection of appropriate research subjects. One of the weakest points of most researchers is insufficient training in experimental design which unintentionally can lead to the implementation of scientifically invalid studies. We should emphasize this in our relevant training so that our experiments are properly designed and executed and our results give no space for doubts about our ethical science.

Informed Consent
Another critical ethical consideration in science is informed consent. This

issue is mainly relevant to research on humans. Informed consent is the process by which individuals are fully informed about the nature of a study and have the opportunity to voluntarily agree to participate. This requires clear and concise explanations of the study's purpose, procedures, risks, and benefits, as well as a clear understanding of the rights of research subjects. Researchers must also ensure that consent is obtained in a manner that is free from coercion or undue influence.

Data Management and Privacy

Data management and privacy are also essential ethical considerations in science. Researchers must take steps to ensure that data is collected, stored, and analyzed in a manner that is both secure and respectful of the privacy and confidentiality of research subjects. This requires careful attention to data security and the use of appropriate safeguards to protect against unauthorized access or disclosure. Contemporary legislation is very strict regarding proper data management and privacy.

Publication and Dissemination

Finally, the publication and dissemination of scientific research raise a range of ethical considerations. Researchers must ensure that their work is accurately and honestly represented in publications and that they appropriately credit the contributions of others. They must also take steps to avoid conflicts of interest and to ensure that their work is used in a manner that is responsible and ethical. Plagiarism is the most common case of unethical behavior in the publication of science.

In summary, I would like to point out that ethics in science is a complex and multifaceted topic that requires careful attention to a range of ethical considerations throughout the scientific process. Scientists must be committed to the responsible conduct of research, obtaining informed consent, protecting data privacy and security, and ensuring that their work is disseminated ethically and responsibly. If we always try to adopt a rigorous and ethical approach to science, we as researchers can help ensure that our work serves the public good and advances our understanding of the world responsibly and ethically.

59 EMBRACING LIFELONG LEARNING: THE KEY TO SUCCESS AND FULFILLMENT

In previous generations, careers probably were simpler: one would graduate from university and then work for a lifetime in the same profession or even in the same company. In present times, it is common to change several employers in our career or even retrain and start a completely new profession. It is a common belief that lifelong learning has become an essential aspect of personal and professional development in today's world. The rapid pace of technological advancements and the ever-changing job market requires individuals to keep themselves updated and acquire new skills constantly. In this section, we will explore the importance of lifelong learning and how it can lead to personal and professional growth.

What is Lifelong Learning?
Lifelong learning refers to the continuous process of acquiring knowledge and skills throughout one's life. It involves formal education, training, self-study, and experiences gained through work and life. Lifelong learning is not limited to a specific age or stage in life, and it is an ongoing process that individuals can engage in at any point in their lives.

Importance of Lifelong Learning
- Personal Growth: Lifelong learning helps individuals to broaden their perspectives, develop critical thinking skills, and become more adaptable to change. It allows individuals to discover new interests, hobbies, and passions and keeps their minds active and engaged.

- Professional Growth: In today's job market, continuous learning is essential for career advancement and job security. Employers value employees who are proactive in their learning and are willing to acquire new skills and knowledge. Lifelong learning also helps individuals to keep up with technological advancements and industry trends, making them more competitive and marketable.

- Social and Cultural Growth: Lifelong learning provides individuals with opportunities to connect with people from different cultures and backgrounds, fostering a deeper understanding and appreciation of diversity.

- Mental Health: Lifelong learning has been linked to improved cognitive function, memory retention, and mental health. It can also reduce the risk of cognitive decline and delay the onset of dementia.

How to Embrace Lifelong Learning
- Be curious: Develop a sense of curiosity about the world around you. Ask questions, seek answers, and explore new ideas.

- Set goals: Set achievable learning goals for yourself and make a plan to achieve them. This could be taking an online course, attending a workshop, or reading a book.

- Stay motivated: Find ways to stay motivated and accountable for your learning. Join a study group, find a learning partner, or track your progress using a learning journal.

- Embrace technology: With the rise of technology, there are countless opportunities for online learning, virtual classes, and webinars. Take advantage of these resources to expand your knowledge and skills.

- Embrace failure: Lifelong learning involves taking risks and stepping out of your comfort zone. Embrace failure as a learning opportunity and use it to improve and grow.

One of the most important messages of this book is that lifelong learning is a crucial aspect of personal and professional development. It provides individuals with opportunities to grow, learn, and adapt to change. Let's all try embracing lifelong learning so that we can achieve personal and professional success, contribute to society, and lead fulfilling lives.

60 MASTERING TIME MANAGEMENT: TECHNIQUES AND STRATEGIES FOR EFFECTIVE PLANNING AND PRODUCTIVITY

It is a paradox that the faster our lives get and the more tools we have to complete tasks in less time, the more we complain about time being not enough! In today's fast-paced world, time management has become an essential skill for everyone. Whether you're a student, a professional, or a business owner, managing your time effectively can make a significant difference in achieving your goals and success. However, the challenge lies in how to manage time efficiently amidst all the distractions and competing demands. Here, I will present to you various techniques and strategies for mastering time management, including goal setting, prioritization, scheduling, delegation, and effective communication.

The first step in effective time management is to set clear and realistic goals. Goals provide direction and motivation, helping you to stay focused on what's important. When setting goals, it's essential to be specific, measurable, achievable, relevant, and time-bound. This way, you can track your progress, celebrate your successes, and adjust your course as needed. For instance, if your goal is to complete a project, break it down into smaller tasks and set deadlines for each task.

Once you have set your goals, the next step is to prioritize your tasks. Not all tasks are equal in terms of importance and urgency, so it's crucial to identify the tasks that will have the most significant impact on your goals. One effective prioritization technique is the Eisenhower Matrix, which categorizes tasks into four quadrants based on their urgency and importance. The tasks in the top left quadrant are the most urgent and important and should be tackled first, while the tasks in the bottom right quadrant are neither urgent nor important and can be eliminated or delegated.

After prioritizing your tasks, it's time to schedule them. Scheduling helps you to allocate your time effectively, ensuring that you have enough time for essential tasks and preventing procrastination. When scheduling, consider your natural rhythms and energy levels. For instance, if you're a morning person, schedule your most critical tasks in the morning when you're most productive. Use tools such as calendars, to-do lists, and time-blocking to plan your day, week, or month.

Delegation is an essential time management skill that many people overlook. Delegating tasks to others can free up your time and energy, allowing you to focus on tasks that require your unique skills and expertise. To delegate effectively, identify tasks that can be delegated, choose the right person for the task, communicate clearly, provide clear instructions and feedback, and trust and empower your team members.

Finally, effective communication is crucial for time management. Miscommunications and misunderstandings can lead to wasted time and unnecessary rework. Therefore, it's essential to communicate clearly and effectively, whether it's with your team, colleagues, or clients. Use active listening skills, ask clarifying questions, provide feedback, and use the appropriate communication channels, whether it's email, phone, or in-person meetings.

We should keep in mind that mastering time management is not a one-size-fits-all solution. It requires experimentation and adaptation to find the techniques and strategies that work best for you. However, it is important to remember that by setting clear goals, prioritizing your tasks, scheduling your time, delegating effectively, and communicating clearly, you can increase your productivity, reduce stress, and achieve your goals with less effort and more satisfaction.

61 ACHIEVE A BALANCE BETWEEN WORK AND PERSONAL LIFE

How many working hours a day are enough for me to achieve a successful career in science? Is it too bad if, in addition to my office workload, I work a couple of hours at home in the afternoon? Could I take advantage of the weekend time to write a scientific paper? Is it ok if I skip spending family time for the benefit of work so that I earn more money for the benefit of the family? Maintaining a healthy balance between work and personal life has become increasingly important in our fast-paced and technology-driven society. With the lines between work and personal life becoming blurred, it has become essential to find a balance that enables us to lead fulfilling and meaningful lives. In the following paragraphs, we will explore the concept of work-life balance and its significance in today's world.

Work-life balance refers to the equilibrium between the time and energy spent on work and personal activities. Achieving balance involves managing one's professional and personal responsibilities in a way that allows for optimal health, happiness, and productivity. The importance of work-life balance has been recognized by both employees and employers, with many companies offering flexible working arrangements and wellness programs to promote a healthier work-life balance for their staff.

We would all agree that maintaining a healthy work-life balance can have numerous benefits. Firstly, it can improve mental health and well-being, reducing the risk of burnout, stress, and anxiety. Secondly, it can enhance job satisfaction and engagement, leading to increased productivity and creativity. Thirdly, it can improve relationships with family and friends, as well as provide opportunities for personal growth and development.

I certainly believe that achieving work-life balance is not always easy, but several strategies can help. Firstly, it is important to set boundaries between work and personal time, such as avoiding checking emails outside of work hours. Secondly, prioritizing activities and tasks can help to manage time more effectively. Thirdly, taking breaks and engaging in leisure activities can help to reduce stress and improve overall well-being. Finally, seeking support from colleagues, friends, and family can help to manage the demands of both work and personal life.

As you may imagine, there are several barriers to achieving work-life balance, including the pressure to work long hours, high workloads, and lack of support from employers. Additionally, technology and social media can make it difficult to disconnect from work and personal obligations, leading to a blurring of boundaries. Recognizing these barriers is the first step in addressing them, and both individuals and organizations need to work together to create a culture that values work-life balance. A scientist's ambition is also an important barrier to achieving a work-life balance because more work commonly delivers more results and faster career advancement.

In summary, I would like to highlight that maintaining a healthy work-life balance is essential for leading a fulfilling and meaningful life. While achieving balance can be challenging, there are several strategies that individuals can employ to manage their time effectively and prioritize their well-being. It is also important for organizations to recognize the importance of work-life balance and implement policies that support their employees' physical, mental, and emotional health. We should try working together, as individuals and organizations so that we can create a culture that values work-life balance and leads to greater happiness and productivity for all.

62 THE INTERCONNECTEDNESS OF MENTAL AND BODY HEALTH

"A healthy mind lives in a healthy body" is a famous slogan suggested by the ancient Roman poet Decimus Junius Juvenalis. A lifestyle of regular body and mind exercise was also popular in ancient Greece. The human body and mind are deeply interconnected, and the health of one is closely linked to the health of the other. A sound mind resides in a healthy body, and a healthy body supports a healthy mind. Mental and physical health are two sides of the same coin, and an imbalance in one can negatively impact the other. Let's discuss the interconnectedness of mental and body health, and how individuals can maintain both for optimal well-being.

Let's first examine body health which refers to the physical state of the body, which includes factors such as nutrition, exercise, sleep, and illness. A healthy body is essential for overall well-being and is the foundation for mental health. Proper nutrition provides the body with the necessary nutrients for energy and growth. Regular exercise helps maintain a healthy weight, improves cardiovascular health, and boosts mood. Sleep is crucial for body repair and rejuvenation, and lack of it can lead to a host of physical and mental health issues. Illness and disease can also impact body health and can negatively impact mental health if left untreated.

On the other hand, mental health refers to the state of a person's emotional, psychological, and social well-being. It is a crucial aspect of overall health and affects how individuals think, feel, and behave. Good mental health includes the ability to cope with stress, maintain healthy relationships, and engage in meaningful activities. Mental health issues can be caused by various factors, including genetics, traumatic experiences, and lifestyle choices. Depression, anxiety, and other mental health disorders can impact physical health by increasing the risk of chronic diseases such as heart disease, diabetes, and obesity.

We could say that the interconnectedness of mental and body health means that an imbalance in one can negatively impact the other. For example, a lack of sleep can negatively impact mental health by increasing the risk of depression, anxiety, and mood disorders. Similarly, chronic stress can negatively impact physical health by increasing the risk of heart disease, stroke, and high blood pressure. A sedentary lifestyle can lead to physical health issues such as obesity, which can negatively impact mental health by increasing the risk of depression and anxiety.

Specialists suggest that to maintain both mental and body health, individuals must focus on several key areas, including:

Nutrition. A balanced and healthy diet is essential for maintaining body health and can also positively impact mental health.

Exercise. Regular physical activity can improve body health and positively impact mental health by boosting mood and reducing stress.

Sleep. Getting enough sleep is crucial for physical and mental health and can help reduce the risk of chronic diseases and mental health disorders.

Stress management. Learning stress management techniques such as meditation, deep breathing, and exercise can help individuals manage stress and improve both physical and mental health.

Social support. Maintaining healthy relationships and engaging in social activities can positively impact mental health and reduce the risk of chronic diseases.

Scientists often put too much pressure on mental activities and neglect physical exercise. Maintaining both mental and body health is essential for overall well-being. The interconnectedness of mental and body health means that an imbalance in one can negatively impact the other. Individuals must focus on maintaining a healthy diet, regular physical activity, adequate sleep, stress management techniques, and social support to maintain optimal well-being. Let's all try prioritizing the combination of mental and body health so that we can lead happy, healthy, and fulfilling lives.

63 TAKE-HOME MESSAGE

As you close this book filled with advice and tips for success in a science career, remember that your path is unique. What worked for one person may not necessarily work for you. Your challenges and circumstances could be different, but that should not deter you from pursuing your dreams.

Science is a constantly evolving field, so it's essential to keep learning and expanding your horizons. Whether it's through attending conferences or workshops, taking online courses, or even reading books like this one, always be open to learning more.

Additionally, remember that setbacks and failures are a part of the journey. Each obstacle you face is an opportunity to learn and grow. Don't be afraid of taking risks, and be willing to pivot and adapt when necessary.

Finally, never forget that science is a collaborative effort. Building a network of supportive colleagues and mentors can make all the difference in your career. Don't be afraid to ask for help and offer support to others as well.

My ultimate take-home message is that to succeed you are advised to work hard. And then work some more. When your supervisor asks you for doing ten tasks, do eleven. When the deadline is in ten days, deliver in nine. Surprise your employers with your extraordinary performance and they will be forced to reward you. Be so good that they cannot afford to lose you.

I hope that the advice in this book will inspire and empower you to reach your full potential in your science career. May your journey be fulfilling, rewarding, and full of discovery.

ABOUT THE AUTHOR

Georgios Koubouris is an accomplished agronomist with years of experience in the field of agriculture. He was born and raised in Greece, where he developed a strong passion for farming and sustainable agriculture at a young age.

After completing his undergraduate degree in agriculture, Georgios went on to earn a master's degree in agronomy, focusing on high-throughput plant propagation. Subsequently, he earned a Ph.D. in plant physiology. He has since dedicated his career to promoting sustainable agriculture practices and improving crop yields in Greece and beyond.

Georgios has worked with a variety of organizations throughout his career, including government agencies, non-profit organizations, and private companies. He has been an invited expert by the European Commission, the National Forestry Academy of China, the International Olive Council, and others. He has conducted research and provided expert advice on topics such as biodiversity, climate change, soil fertility, and food quality.

Georgios is known for his innovative approach to agriculture, always looking for new and improved ways to help farmers increase their yields while minimizing their environmental impact. He has also been a vocal advocate for the importance of sustainable agriculture practices, both in Greece and on a global scale.

Currently, he is the Lead Researcher at the Olive Growing Laboratory in the Institute for Olive Tree, Subtropical Crops and Viticulture at the Hellenic Agricultural Organization ELGO DIMITRA, Greece. He has published more than 70 papers in international scientific journals indexed in SCOPUS, participated in over 40 research projects, and managed grants for over 2M€. He has acted as a scientific leader of the project Oliveclima which was awarded as the best project for climate action in Europe by the European Commission, LIFE, 2019. He is a member of the editorial boards of the international scientific journals "Frontiers in Plant Science", "Plan3ts-MDPI", "Sustainability-MDPI", "International Journal of Plant Biology MDPI", "Genetic Resources" and "Vegetos - Springer Nature" while in the past he also served "Experimental Agriculture-Cambridge University Press".

In addition to his work as an agronomist, Georgios is also a respected educator, sharing his knowledge and expertise with the next generation of farmers and agronomists. He has published numerous articles and research papers in leading agricultural journals and has presented his findings at conferences and seminars around the world. He also participates in the editorial boards of some of the most prestigious scientific journals in the world.

Georgios's contributions to the field of agriculture have been recognized by his peers and colleagues, and he has received numerous awards and honors throughout his career. He continues to be an influential figure in the world of sustainable agriculture and a passionate advocate for the importance of responsible farming practices.